Starting with Turkeys

Katie Thear

d Leys Publishing Ltd

Starting with Turkeys

First edition published by Broad Leys Publishing Ltd 2007.

A catalogue record for this book is available from the British Library.

ISBN: 978 0 9061 3740 6

Outside front cover: Bronze turkey stag

Outside back: *Top* - Lavender stag
                  Middle - Cröllwitzer stag and hen
                  Bottom - Buff hen

Unless stated otherwise the photographs were taken by the author.

For details of our other publications please see page 96.

Broad Leys Publishing Ltd
1 Tenterfields,
Newport, Saffron Walden,
Essex CB11 3UW, UK.
Tel/Fax: 01799 541065
E-mail: kdthear@btinternet.com
Website: www.blpbooks.co.uk

Contents

Preface

When turkeys approach they alert you in their noisy, gobbly fashion.
(Raising Your Own Turkeys. Leonard Mercia. 1981)

My parents never kept turkeys on their small farm, so it was not until I had my own smallholding that I first kept these large birds. I suppose I had the idea that they were like chickens, only bigger. However, I was soon to discover that they are characters in their own right.

At that time, virtually all turkeys were intensively reared and the only way that we were able to acquire some young birds was to ask a nearby producer if we could buy a dozen of his poults the next time he had a delivery of day-olds. Laughingly he agreed, but was incredulous when we told him that we intended to rear them on free-range. *'They'll never survive'*, he predicted, but they did, and what's more, they flourished!

Since those days, it has become more common for all poultry, including turkeys, to be reared in outside conditions. There has also been a welcome and renewed interest in the traditional breeds.

This book is therefore aimed at those who are interested in keeping the traditional breeds of turkeys on a small scale. They may be those who wish to rear free-range or organic birds for Christmas, in order to supply local markets, or they may wish to show and promote the old breeds. I hope that anyone interested in turkeys will find something useful in the book.

(Katie Thear, Newport. 2007)

Acknowledgements

I am very grateful to the following for their invaluable help in the production of this book, which includes advice and the loan of photographs, as well as in some cases, welcoming me to their farms.

Janice Houghton Wallace, Turkey Club UK

Bernie and Clive Landshoff, Domestic Fowl Trust

Kelly Turkey Farms

Norfolk Rare Breeds Centre

Peele's Norfolk Black Turkeys

Robert Stephenson

Brian Hale

University of Leeds

Introduction

To begin at the beginning
(Under Milkwood. Dylan Thomas. 1956)

It's always best to begin at the beginning and to ask why anyone would want to keep turkeys. An interest is, of course, a prerequisite, but there are other factors involved. Perhaps the most crucial is to establish whether there are any conditions or restrictions that apply to turkeys?

Are there any restrictions?

As with most things, there are regulations but they are not as tiresome as some would have us believe. They are there to protect the interests of the consumer, flock health and welfare, and ultimately the reputation of the breeder and supplier.

Poultry Register

Anyone with fifty or more birds, or is involved with a commercial enterprise, must register with *DEFRA*. This is part of the health regulations that came in after the concerns about avian influenza.

To register, call the Freephone 0800 634 1112. Lines are open 8am to 8pm, Monday to Friday, and 9am to 1pm, on Saturday and Sunday. It is also possible to download a form from the *DEFRA* website at www.defra.gov.uk

Registration of a breeding flock

If you have 250 or more turkeys in a breeding flock, it is necessary to be registered and to take regular samples for salmonella checking. If you are already registered with *DEFRA*, as above, it may not be necessary to do it again, but you need to check in case they do not have all the details.

An application form is available from *DEFRA* or from the *Local Animal Health Office*. Once registered, a registration number is issued to the owner of the breeding flock.

Most small turkey breeders will not be involved with this registration and with salmonella checks because the numbers they keep are usually far fewer than 250 breeding birds.

Free-range regulations

If turkeys are sold as free-range, it is necessary to provide suitable access to outside conditions and to meet the conditions specified by the regulations. These are discussed later in the book.

Organic regulations

Where turkeys are sold as 'organic', the producer must be registered with an appropriate organic certification organisation such as the *Soil Association* or *Organic Farmers and Growers*. All the organic requirements in relation to housing, flock density, feeding, land use and management must be complied with. (See page 73).

Slaughtering and processing regulations

Depending on the scale and nature of the enterprise, there are regulations that are concerned with welfare, health and safety. Further information is provided in the *Christmas Turkeys* chapter.

What else should be considered?

Turkeys are big birds and there are occasions when it will be necessary to pick them up. Although they are not normally aggressive, it is not sensible to keep turkeys if there is a lack of confidence in handling them, or if someone has an allergy to feathers. Incidentally, the correct way to pick up a turkey is to do so gently and unhurriedly, while restraining the wings and supporting the bird from beneath, as shown opposite.

There needs to be enough house and run space for the number of birds envisaged: newly hatched poults soon grow into large birds! Allowance should also be made for the rotation of land, with new areas of grazing being made available on a regular basis. Not to do so is to risk the possibility of disease from over-used land. Flock densities are looked at later in the book.

It is also important that chickens should not have had access to the land because of the danger of blackhead disease to which turkeys are particularly susceptible. Chickens can carry this without being affected by it.

Secure storage areas for food and floor litter such as wood shavings will also be required, as well as an appropriate building for housing an incubator and brooder, if breeding of replacement birds is to take place.

If farm-fresh turkeys are to be sold, further areas may also be required. These aspects are explored later in the book.

Finding out about turkeys before acquiring them is obviously recommended. Poultry shows often have displays of the various breeds and it is a good opportunity to talk to the breeders as well as viewing the birds.

The *Poultry Club of Great Britain* protects the interests of the various breeds and publishes the standards for them. These list the ideal points of each breed, thus providing a standard template against which individual birds can be measured.

The *Turkey Club UK*, which is affiliated to the *Poultry Club*, is an organisation specifically for those who are interested in turkeys. As with the *Poultry Club*, the emphasis is on the traditional breeds.

The correct way to hold a turkey is to restrain the wings and support it from below. *(Katie Thear)*

Keeping traditional breeds and promoting them at poultry shows helps to conserve them at a time when some have become endangered. Most commercial turkeys have been developed to the extent that they are now so large that they can no longer mate naturally and so artificial insemination has to be used. Most commercial turkeys are also white-feathered because it was perceived that housewives wanted carcases without black feather stubs.

In recent years there has been a reversal of this attitude, with coloured turkeys becoming associated with free-range and less intensive systems. Locally produced turkeys are also becoming more popular at Christmas, particularly where customers are able to order in advance. A turkey that is slower-growing will fit comfortably into their ovens, rather than a gargantuan creature that would feed a whole restaurant!

There are many reasons for keeping turkeys, including conserving the old breeds, supplying a local demand for free-range and organic birds at Christmas, as well as showing and keeping a few birds as pets.

Whatever the reasons, these big birds will thrive if they are given the care and attention that they deserve, and that are outlined in the free *DEFRA* publication *Codes of Recommendation for the Welfare of Livestock: Turkeys*.

Turkeys through the Ages

Depiction of the turkey
in an Aztec motif.
(16th century)

Miniature painting. Mogul period of
Shah Jehan. *(Fitzwilliam Museum,
Cambridge. 17th Century)*

American Wild Turkey.
(John Audabon. 19th Century).

Bronze turkeys in England.
(Harrison Weir.1860)

Norfolk Blacks. *(Ludlow. 19th Century)*

Bronze turkeys, England 1930s.

The turkey honoured
on a Mexican stamp.

About the Turkey

History of turkeys

Exactly how and where the turkey evolved initially will probably never be known, but bone remains dating back to 11,000BC have been discovered in Mexico and Central America, and this seems the most likely area from which they spread to other areas of the American continent, such as the Fort Rock Basin of the USA where prehistoric remains have also been unearthed.

The Aztecs called them Huexolotlin and used turkey feathers for decoration. They were regarded as a manifestation of the god Tezcatlipoca (the trickster) in whose honour two feasts a year were held. The Aztecs also domesticated the turkey. When this occurred is unknown, but 2000 - 3000BC is a period thought to be the most likely, as far as the evidence of prehistoric artefacts indicates.

When the Spanish Conquistadores, under the command of Hermán Cortés, arrived in Mexico in 1519, they found that the Aztec Emperor Montezuma had turkeys in his aviaries, with some being used to feed the royal eagles. Many were also eaten at Aztec feasts and the feathers were used in head dresses, cloaks and for fletching arrows. Bernard Diaz, a Spanish soldier, recorded that at a royal feast: *'They cooked 300 plates of food - fowls and turkeys - that the great Montezuma was to eat.'*

From 1519 onwards, turkeys were brought back to Spain in appreciable numbers, although a few had been introduced earlier. In 1500, the sailor Pedro Alonso Niño had returned to Spain with a few birds. Christopher Columbus had also been given some at Honduras in 1502. There are additional Spanish references to some being introduced to Seville in 1512. From Spain they quickly spread to other areas of Europe and the East.

In Spain, turkeys were usually referred to as Indian fowl. This was on the basis that their name for Central America was the Spanish Indies. 1524 is the first date when they were recorded as having reached Britain and they were referred to by the name we call them today.

William Strickland, on a voyage to the New World, is said to have brought back turkeys and in 1550 his coat of arms included a turkey stag. At first, they must have been available in limited numbers only, for in 1541 Archbishop Cranmer prohibited the serving of more than one turkey at state occasions, on the basis that there was a shortage of breeding stock.

Points of a Turkey as shown in a Bronze Stag

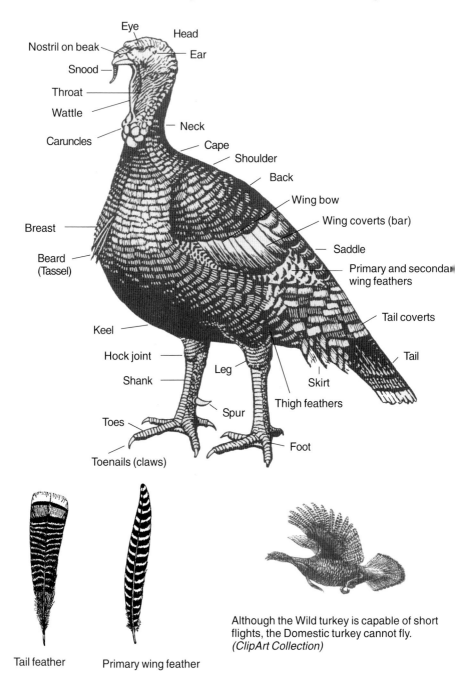

Tail feather

Primary wing feather

Although the Wild turkey is capable of short flights, the Domestic turkey cannot fly.
(ClipArt Collection)

By 1573 however, the situation had obviously improved because Tusser was able to report that Christmas in England meant: *'Beef, mutton and port, shred pies of the best, pig, veal, goose and capon, and turkey well drest'*.

Turkeys were served at the wedding of Charles XI of France to Elizabeth of Austria in 1570, and the king subsequently established a breeding flock of them in the forest of St Germain.

In the 18th century, George II established a flock of 3,000 turkeys in Richmond Park, while Coke of Norfolk (the Earl of Leicester) also had a flock at Holkham Park.

The turkey's association with feasting and plenty, and the male's strutting display posture, may well have been why Peter Bruegel the Elder used them as a symbol of envy in his 1557 drawing *Fortitude*. In this, the turkey is shown being slain as one of the seven deadly sins.

Turkeys may have been the festive choice for the wealthy, but goose continued to be the prime Christmas bird in Britain until the 19th century. It was only after the novel *The Christmas Carol* by Charles Dickens was published in 1843 that the turkey began to be the festive bird of choice. Even so, the turkey did not become the Christmas bird in many parts of Britain, such as Wales, until much later. I was 21 years of age before I ever tasted turkey!

From the early 17th century, many settlers, amongst them the Pilgrim Fathers, took turkeys with them from Britain and other parts of Europe to the Americas. These then crossed with wild turkeys found in the wooded areas of the new world. The name Bronze turkey was first used in Port Judith, Rhode Island, 1830, after Narragansett turkeys were crossed with wild stock.

Some of these hybrids were, in turn, brought back to England, where a gamekeeper called John Bull began to select them for a broader breast. He subsequently emigrated to Canada, taking some of his stock with him, and sold some of the broad breasted birds to North America. Breeding for massive birds was to continue in the USA from then on until the present-day.

The New Englanders of the eastern seaboard of America understandably adopted turkeys as the chief menu item for their annual thanksgiving feast, but when the fourth Thursday in November was officially adopted as a national day of thanksgiving in 1863, not everyone agreed with the choice of another bird as the nation's symbol; the bald-headed eagle.

Benjamin Franklin, in a letter written to his daughter, was of the view that the turkey was a more appropriate American symbol than the bald-headed eagle. *'The turkey is a much more respectable bird and withal a true native of North America.'*

However, the choice is perhaps understandable. What nation really wants to be thought of as a turkey?

(Incidentally, the bald-headed eagle is not really bald; it has a white head and is so-called because of its 'piebald' black and white colouring).

Classification

If we 'place' turkeys in the classification system devised by Linnaeus in the 18th century, and which is being constantly updated, their position in relation to the rest of the bird kingdom is as follows:

Class: *Aves* (Birds)
Order: *Galliformes* (Game birds and fowl)
Genus: *Meleagrididae* (Turkeys)
Species: *Meleagris gallopavo* (Wild Bush/North American turkey)

        Sub-species: *M.g. silvestris* (Eastern wild turkey)
                  M.g. osceola (Florida wild turkey)
                  M.g. intermedia (Rio Grande wild turkey)
                  M.g. merriamis (Merriam's wild turkey)
                  M.g. mexicani (Gould's wild turkey)

Species: *Meleagris ocellata* (Mexican wild turkey)

Wild turkeys

There are two species of wild turkey, the Wild Bush or North American, *Meleagris gallopavo*, and the Ocellated or Mexican wild turkey, *Meleagris ocellata*.

Wild Bush or North American

The Wild North American or Bush turkey, *Meleagris gallopavo*, is the species from which most of our domestic turkeys have evolved and have been developed subsequently. There are five sub-species associated with the different geographical areas of North America. They show variations in size, plumage colour and markings.

Over-hunting virtually wiped out wild turkeys in many areas of the USA, but since the 1960s efforts have been made to reintroduce them. Hunting is now regulated and restricted to certain times of the year. Even so, the advice I received in Kansas was not to go for a stroll in the woods wearing turkey colours, or to make any turkey calls, otherwise I was likely to be shot! To play safe, I kept quiet and stayed in town!

It is now virtually impossible to know what crossings, natural or intended, were responsible for producing the various sub-species. As referred to earlier, the first settlers took European stock with them. These were originally turkeys brought by the Conquistadores from the New World to Spain and then selectively bred for increased body weight in different European countries such as England and Holland. These re-introductions would almost certainly have inter-bred with the indigenous wild populations.

The sub-species that are now found are as follows:

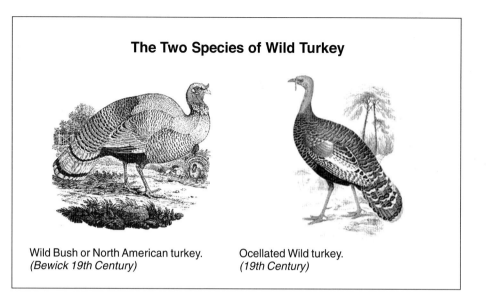

The Two Species of Wild Turkey

Wild Bush or North American turkey.
(Bewick 19th Century)

Ocellated Wild turkey.
(19th Century)

Eastern Wild Turkey *(Meleagris gallopavo silvestris)*
This is thought to be closest to the type found by the early American settlers in the 17th century. It is dark bronze in colour with a brown rump and tail margins. There is black and white barring across the primary and secondary feathers so that when the wings are folded, the secondaries look as if they have white triangular patches. It was crossed with the European Black to produce turkeys that were eventually to form the basis of the future turkey industry.

Florida Wild Turkey *(Meleagris gallopavo osceola)*
This is similar to the Eastern but the triangular patches of the secondary feathers are absent and there is more black than white in the barring.

Rio Grande Wild Turkey *(Meleagris gallopavo intermedia)*
This variety has tail feathers tipped in white rather than brown.

Merriam's Wild Turkey *(Meleagris gallopavo merriama)*
Found in the Rocky Mountains, this has white back and tail feathers.

Gould's Wild Turkey *(Meleagris gallopavo mexicana)*
Common in the mountainous regions of Mexico, but rare in the USA, this is the largest wild turkey.

A small, all-black turkey, *Meleagris gallopavo gallopavo*, is historically accepted as being the sub-species that the Conquistadores took back to Spain in the 16th century, to become the ancestor of the European Black turkey, but if it still exists in the wild, it has yet to be established.

Oscellated Wild Turkey

The Oscellated wild turkey, *Meleagris ocellata*, is a separate species, as referred to earlier, and is only found in Mexico. It is the smallest wild turkey and gets its name from the 'ocelli' or peacock-like eye markings on the tail feathers. Outside Central America it is regarded as a rare aviary bird. As far as is known, there are no sub-species.

Domesticated breeds

It is probable that some degree of domestication of wild turkeys took place amongst the indigenous native American tribes before Europeans arrived, although there is comparatively little evidence to support this. However, not all the tribes were nomadic, as previously supposed. Archaeological excavations have found remains of permanent settlements with many turkey bones on the sites. The Aztecs too, are thought to have domesticated them.

However, ongoing and consistent domestication did not take place until the Europeans arrived in the Americas. The breeds that were subsequently developed and are available today are detailed in the next chapter on *Breeds*.

Characteristics of turkeys

Whether they are wild or domesticated, turkeys share the same basic characteristics. Having a knowledge of what these are makes it easier to provide conditions that are suitable for them.

Predator protection

In the wild, turkeys inhabit forested or partially wooded areas that provide protection against predators. In a domestic situation such protection still provides a sense of security, even though the turkeys may not be at risk. They can be frightened by aircraft or by any loud noises. Tree or hedging cover also provides shade and wind protection.

The reaction to fear can elicit several responses, including freezing, loud alarm calling (see page 19), running away or vigorous flapping of the wings.

The area where the turkeys are ranging needs to be well fenced against foxes for it is untrue that they are too big for foxes to take. Strong fencing to a height of 2m will normally keep out foxes, especially if there is an added overhang of 30cm extending outwards at the top. Alternatively, electric fencing is effective in deterring them.

Ground orientated

The turkey is essentially a ground orientated bird, although it has retained the perching instinct as a survival mechanism. The Wild Bush turkey is capable of short bursts of flight but the domestic breeds have lost the ability, athough they are capable of running quite quickly as well as flapping their

Norfolk Black and Bronze growers on free-range but with substantial fencing to keep them safe from foxes, as well as tree cover for wind protection and a sense of security. *(Katie Thear)*

way up to a perch. As ground-orientated birds, they also make their nests at ground level in the wild. For this, a well sheltered, protected and private area is required.

Scratching and pecking

They spend a great deal of their time searching and scratching about for food. Their eyesight is good and their feet and toes are well adapted for raking about in the ground cover.

They are naturally omnivorous, taking in plants, seeds, insects and worms. The beak is a necessary instrument for this as it is well equipped with sensory cells. Beak trimming, which is often carried out in large flocks, diminishes the natural ability to forage. In small, well managed flocks, it is neither necessary nor humane to beak-trim.

In research carried out by Rachel Crowe and Michael Forbes at the University of Leeds, CDs were suspended in a turkey house and provided the turkeys with a diversion so that they were less likely to peck each other. It was also possible to have stronger lighting in the house as a result.

Ref: Crowe & Forbes. Reporter 444. University of Leeds. December 1999).

Research has shown that providing hanging objects such as unwanted CDs helps to prevent turkeys pecking each other. *(University of Leeds)*

Perching

As referred to earlier, the domestic turkey is descended from a wild wood-land perching bird so perches are required. These should be available both in the house and outside.

Stepped perches are acceptable but the lower one should be no more than 45cm from the ground, with a minimum of 40cm perch space allowed per bird. The ideal width of perch for the foot to grasp is 8cm, with the surface being slightly rounded.

Straw bales also make acceptable perching areas and many rearers prefer to use these in case distortion of the breastbone results. (See *Crooked keel*, Page 20).

Preening

Like most birds, turkeys will preen and groom their feathers to keep them in good condition. A certain amount of oil is deposited on the feathers from the preen gland at the base of the tail, but it is not enough to make the plumage totally weatherproof, as it is with waterfowl. Substantial, easily accessible shelter is therefore essential.

Preening also 'combs' the feathers so that they are kept in good condition. Any bird that neglects to preen itself so that the feathers become increasingly unsightly should be checked in case it is ill. Bear in mind, however, that during the moulting period of the breeding birds, when old feathers are shed to be replaced by new ones, the plumage can look ragged and unsightly

Commercial White turkeys in an open-fronted barn that has straw bales provided as perches.
(Brian Hale)

Dust-bathing

Dust-bathing is an instinctive pattern of behaviour where the birds shuffle and roll about in fine soil, allowing it to trickle through the feathers in an attempt to dislodge any external parasites. If there is an infestation of such parasites, then action needs to be taken to deal with them, rather than relying on dustbaths. (See *External Parasites* Page 84).

Even if the birds are clear of parasites, they will often indulge in dust-bathing so it is important that appropriate conditions are available to them. Free-ranging turkeys will often establish where their dust-baths are situated. Alternatively, an area of fine sand with weather protection can be provided.

Courtship behaviour

There's no mistaking the courtship behaviour of the stags! In the wild they establish territories or strutting areas. The domestic turkey is no exception. His face, snood, wattles and caruncles become red and he struts around displaying his tail feathers while gobbling and puffing. As well as being raised in display, the tail feathers are vibrated, producing a characteristic whirring sound.

Very heavy commercial hybrids are no longer able to mate naturally so artificial insemination has to be used instead. This is yet another reason why the traditional breeds are more appropriate for the small farmer who wishes to produce replacement stock.

As a perching bird, the turkey appreciates perches inside and outside. Electrified poultry netting at the back provides protection against foxes while the trees act as a windbreak. *(Katie Thear)*

Here, the outside perches have added weather protection. *(Katie Thear)*

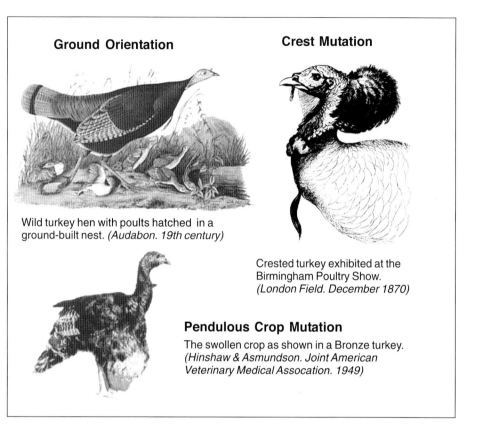

Ground Orientation

Wild turkey hen with poults hatched in a ground-built nest. *(Audabon. 19th century)*

Crest Mutation

Crested turkey exhibited at the Birmingham Poultry Show. *(London Field. December 1870)*

Pendulous Crop Mutation

The swollen crop as shown in a Bronze turkey. *(Hinshaw & Asmundson. Joint American Veterinary Medical Assocation. 1949)*

Calls

Turkeys have a whole series of calls that are associated with alarm, social interaction within the flock, and courtship. The main ones are as follows but I am sure that there are many more whose interpretation is unknown to us:

Gobble: This is produced by the male as part of his courtship display and to establish dominance over any rivals in a particular territory. It is also apparent when there is any disturbance to the flock.

Phutt: A loud alarm call when danger is sensed.

Drumming: This is a two note puffing sound from the stag used as part of his courtship display to attract females.

Purr: A soft sound produced by both sexes when they feed or when they are communicating with each other.

Loud purr: An aggressive rattling sound produced by the male as he gets ready to fight a rival.

Cluck: A staccato sound used by both sexes to communicate with each other. A series of continuous loud clucks is a distress call from a hen that has become separated from the others.

Yelp: A rhythmic and continuous sound used to locate other turkeys, emitted by both males and females. A shorter, softer note from this is often used in the morning, to indicate that all is well.

Cackle: A sound emitted by the female when she goes up to or down from the roost. It is usually followed by clucks when she reaches the ground.

Peep peep: A whistling sound from newly hatched birds.

Kee kee: A note emitted by the young poult as it gets older.

Kee kee run: The sound produced by the poult as it nears adulthood.

Mutations
Random genetic mutations occur in all life forms and the turkey is no exception. Some genes are lethal in their effects, while others are benign.

Crest mutation
The appearance of a crest as a protuberance of the skull is known to appear as a rare condition. It is similar to the crest of other poultry such as that of the Crested duck. A Crested turkey was exhibited at the *Birmingham Poultry Show* in 1870. There is also a reference by a Mr Wilmot to Crested turkeys in the *Gardener's Chronicle* of 1852: '*A white turkey-cock had a crest formed of feathers about four inches long, with bare quills, and a tuft of soft white down growing at the end. Many of the young birds inherited this kind of crest, but afterwards it fell off or was pecked out by the other birds*'.

Crooked keel
When turkeys are found to have crooked breastbones, it is often thought to be the result of distortion as a result of using perches. Many rearers therefore prefer to use straw bales. It should be remembered however, that there is a gene for faulty bone development, and that the use of perches may merely be extending the extent to which the hereditary weakness is expressed.
(Ref: Nieman 1931, Warren 1937, Biegert 1937).

Short spine
This is where the neck and body are markedly short as a result of the vertebrae being crowded together, although the head may be normal. It is caused by a recessive gene that is invariably lethal, usually in the shell in the later stages of incubation. (Ref: Asmundson 1942)

Short 'long' bones
Caused by another recessive gene, this condition produces leg bones that are shorter but thicker than normal ones. Most affected birds die, but around 3% survive to maturity although they have difficulty in walking and are not capable of mating. (Ref: Asmundson 1944).

Bronze stag displaying. *(Katie Thear)*

Imperfect albinism

This is a recessive, sex-linked condition where melanin is missing in parts of the eye, although it may be apparent elsewhere. It often results in blindness. Poults that are not humanely killed at hatch usually die within a few weeks so the gene may be regarded as semi-lethal. Where the birds do survive, the plumage is dingy white with some pigmentation. (Ref: Hutt and Muller 1942)

Pendulous crop

This is caused by a recessive gene and produces a distended crop in which liquid tends to accumulate. As with all undesirable genetic traits, it is important not to breed from affected birds. (Ref: Asmundson & Hinshaw 1938).

Colour mutations

The basic plumage colour of the turkey is bronze, such as that found in the Wild Bush turkey. All the colour variations are mutations that have led to the development of different varieties of turkeys. Where these varieties are then selected until they breed true (the young always resemble the parents), they are then designated as standardised breeds. Further information on colour mutations will be found in the following chapter on *Breeds*.

Young Norfolk Black stag. *(Katie Thear)*

French Black stag. The plumage is more glossy than that of the Norfok Black. *(Katie Thear)*

Breeds

Contemplation makes a rare turkey cock of him.

(Twelfth Night. William Shakespeare)

An iridescent green bronze is the standard plumage colour pattern in the wild turkey from which the domestic bird is derived. Genetic variations in which bronze is replaced by other pigmentations have given rise to the other breeds that have since been standardised.

Depending on their genetic colour inheritance, domestic turkeys can be regarded as belonging to one of the following six groups: Bronze, Black, White, Blue, Red or Pied. Depending on their size and weight, they may also be classified as light or heavy.

There is arguably no such thing as a truly pure breed for they are all originally developed from a variety of crossings based on the wild turkey, but it is used to describe a breed that has been standardised to the extent that the young always resemble the parents when two of the same breed are mated.

Standardised breeds

At the time of writing, the following breeds are those that are recognised as standardised breeds in Britain and the USA:

Britain (*British Poultry Standards*): Bronze, Cambridge Bronze, Crimson Dawn, Norfolk Black, British White, Slate, Bourbon Red, Buff, Cröllwitzer.

USA (*American Standard of Perfection*): Bronze, Black, White Holland, Beltsville Small White, Narragansett, Slate, Bourbon Red, Royal Palm.

Within Europe, most of these breeds are available, although they often have their own names as well as slightly differing standards, depending on the country and the breed organisations. There are also variations in details between the British and the American standards.

Some of the breeds have locally-produced strains that differ in their range of plumage colour. Some may be the result of spontaneous genetic mutation, but most derive from crosses and are not recognised as standardised breeds. Hybrids have also been developed for commercial purposes.

Bronze turkeys

Bronze

This old established breed is the closest in colouring to the indigenous wild turkey of the USA. It was originally bred in 1830, in Port Judith, Rhode Island, by crossing the Narrangansett with wild turkeys of the area. It was recognised as a standardised breed in the USA in 1874.

23

In Britain the Bronze is recognised as one of the heavy standardised breeds. As the name indicates, plumage is bronze in colour with a metallic sheen.

It has black and white flight feathers, and a black, brown and white edged tail. All-white feathers are regarded as a fault in the breed standards for all the bronze breeds.

Finished weights for the stag are 13.6 - 18kg. Those for a hen are 8 - 12kg. The finished weights represent the birds at maturity. Those slaughtered for the Christmas market will normally be 18 - 25% lighter when oven-ready.

Cambridge Bronze

Recognised in the *British Poultry Standards* as a heavy breed, this is smaller than the Bronze, with mature stags at 8.1 - 10.8kg, and hens at 5.4 - 7.25kg. The plumage is duller in hue than the Bronze, and the body feathers are tipped with grey or white in both sexes. Feet and legs are dark grey, while the beak may be flesh coloured or horn. The eyes are dark brown.

Edward Brown, writing in 1906, was of the view that the Cambridge Bronze had been bred from crossings of the Norfolk Black and the American Bronze, but he was at pains to point out that while the Bronze was heavier, the meat was not of the same quality as that of the Norfolk Black.

Crimson Dawn (Black-Winged Bronze)

This heavy breed is derived from a genetic variation where the bird has the typical bronze colour and plumage pattern, but the primary wing feathers are completely black without barring. The secondary feathers are white-tipped black. In all other features, including weights, the Crimson Dawn is the same as the Bronze. The breed standards permit a certain amount of white on the shoulders.

Broad Breasted Bronze

Commercial interests in the USA developed the Broad Breasted Bronze, probably based on John Bull's past introductions via Canada, referred to on Page 11. This, in turn, came back to Britain as one of the best-selling commercial breeds until ousted by the development of the White.

In recent years, the Broad-Breasted Bronze has found a growing market in the UK as a quality bird reared on grass for the farm-fresh Christmas market. Today there are considerable numbers of commercial Bronze turkeys reared in the UK. These are hybridised strains that have been developed from the traditional breeds for specific markets. *Kelly Turkey Farms*, for example, supply the heavy Wrolstad Bronze, the medium sized Roly Poly Bronze and the small Super Mini Bronze. These enable producers to rear to the weight range that customers want.

Farmers also adopt different rearing and feeding regimes, including the production of organically reared turkeys.

Buff hen. *(Katie Thear)*

Cröllwitzer hen. *(Katie Thear)*

Narrangansett

In the Narrangansett, the bronze colour is genetically replaced by steel-grey, although the grey colouration does not become apparent until the birds are between six and eight weeks of age.

The breed was originally developed in the Narrangansett Bay area of Rhode Island in the USA. Black turkeys brought by the early settlers were crossed with Eastern wild turkeys. It became an important meat bird in New England, but the numbers declined as the Broad Breasted Bronze and commercial White turkeys came to the fore after the 1900s.

It was first recognised by the *American Poultry Association* in 1874 but at the time of writing, has not yet been recognised in the British Standards for its numbers here are still relatively low.

The colouring is broadly of grey black bands to the feathers with some bronze in places. The covert wings are pale grey with black tips and the secondaries are of alternate black and white bars. The finished weight for a stag is around 15kg, while that for a hen is around 8.2kg.

Silver Narrangansett: This is a variety of the Narrangansett where the steel grey is replaced by white in the plumage.

Black Turkeys

Norfolk Black (Black Norfolk)

The Norfolk Black is almost certainly the oldest British turkey breed. The original black turkeys were probably derived from those first brought to Europe from Central America by the Spanish Conquistadores. In East Anglia they were developed as a meat breed and were subsequently reintroduced to the United States by the early settlers. There, they formed the basis of the American Black.

Crosses with the Bronze turkey in the past to improve the Norfolk Black's size and vigour, means that many birds now have some bronze colouring on the back and tail. The breed standards regard these as faults. In both sexes the plumage is black all over with a red head and face, while the legs, feet and beak are also black. It is classified as a light breed. Finished weight for a mature stag is around 11.4kg, and for a hen, 5.9 – 6.8kg.

There are some strains of Norfolk Black turkeys raised commercially for the Farm Fresh market.

American Black

In the USA, this is referred to as the Black. It was first recognised as a standardised breed in 1874. It is generally heavier than the Norfolk Black, with mature stags at 14.9kg, while hens are around 8.1kg.

Blue/Slate hen. *(Katie Thear)*

Broad Breasted White turkeys being reared on free-range in New England. *(Katie Thear)*

Pavo de Negra
This is the small black turkey of Spain that is descended from the original introductions by the Conquistadores.

French Black
The French Black is of the same origin, but this and Pavo de Negra have much more lustrous black plumage than the Norfolk Black, which tends to be more matt and dull by comparison.

White turkeys

British White
Originally a mutation of the black, the White seems to have been developed in Europe. It was first documented in the UK in the early 1800s.

From Europe, it was introduced to the USA as the White Holland, indicating its place of origin. There are also past references to an Austrian White in the USA, indicating that there were several European sources.

It was first recognised as the White Holland in the USA in 1874. It is heavier than the British White. Commercial development there also subsequently hybridised it to produce the Broad-Breasted or Large White.

In Britain the only recognised and standardised breed of white turkey is the British White which is a heavy breed. The plumage is all white, apart from the tassel which is black. The legs and feet are flesh-coloured, while the

Blue/Slate stag. *(Norfolk Rare Breeds Centre)*.

face, caruncles and wattles are bright red, although these can vary to blue and white in the stag. The beak is a pale horn colour.

Finished weight of the mature British White stag is around 12.7kg, while that of the hen is 7.3 – 10kg.

Broad Breasted White

The main breed used for intensive, commercial production is the Broad-Breasted White, noted for its quick growth and high meat to bone ratio. Some of these birds can grow to such large sizes that natural mating is impossible, so artificial insemination must be used. The very large strains are also prone to leg problems, especially if they do not exercise in free-ranging conditions.

Most small producers tend to concentrate on the more traditional and slower-growing breeds that are more appropriate for outside conditions. However, there has been more emphasis in recent years on producing birds of differing maxi, midi and mini sizes, and other characteristics for the varied needs of the turkey market. These are often given specific names by their breeders. *Kelly Turkey Farms*, for example, produces the Super Mini White, the RolyPoly White and the Wrolstad Plumpie.

Beltsville White

During the 1930s the Beltsville Small White was developed in the USA, in Beltsville, Maryland as a small commercial white turkey. It grew steadily in popularity, with numbers peaking in the 1950s when they began to be ousted

A young Norfolk Black hen. *(Katie Thear)*

by the quicker growing strains of the Broad-Breasted White. It is a standardised breed in the USA, having been recognised as such in 1951. There, the required characteristics are: pure white plumage, red head and thoat, pinkish white legs and feet, and horn beak. The standard weight for a mature stag is 9.5kg, while that for a hen is 5.4kg. An excess over this of 1.36kg for the stag and 0.9kg for the hen results in a disqualification from the standards. It is not yet recognised as a standardised breed in Britain.

Midget White

During the early 20th century American breeders developed the Midget White, which also in its turn declined in numbers before the competition. It is still bred by a few breeders in the USA, although it is not recognised anywhere as a standardised breed.

Nebraskan

The Nebraskan Spotted turkey is essentially a white bird with black, brown or buff speckling. They are very rare and there are currently few in the UK.

Blue Turkeys

Slate (Blue)

Classified as a light breed in the *British Poutry Standards*, the Slate or Blue is a breed with a distinctive colour that originated as a genetic mutation of the black turkey, where there is a reduction in the black pigmentation. The breed was first recognised by the *American Poultry Association* in 1874. and a small number of American Slate turkeys are to be found in Britain.

In the early 20th century Edward Brown called the Slate turkey, the Grey, pointing out that it was common in Cambridge and Norfolk where it was called the Bustard turkey. He also referred to its high qualities as a table bird in Ireland and expressed the wish that it should be further developed there. Alas, it never was.

The British and American standards both specify an all-over, even shade of slate colour that is free of contrasting dark feathers. This is sometimes referred to as the Self Blue and is acceptable as a light or dark shade of slate, as long as the colouring is even. The lighter version is often referred to as the Lavender.

The beak, feet and legs are also slate blue, while the face, wattles and caruncles should be as red as possible. The eyes are dark. It can be difficult to breed good examples of the breed, and there are often dark flecks within the colour (see below). Older birds can also develop red in the tail. Finished weights for a stag are 8.2 – 11.3kg, and for the hen 6.4 – 8.2kg.

Just to complicate things, there are two slate/blue genes, one dominant and one recessive. The former produces a slate-blue colour with barred wings and tail feathers. The latter produces a darker slate colour with barred flight feathers and pencilled tail feathers. They are not currently recognised as standard breeds. Some blue/slate turkeys have recently been introduced successfully to the UK Christmas market.

Brown turkeys

Buff

Here, the typical bronze plumage colour is genetically replaced by a red-brown pigmentation. It was recognised by the *American Poultry Association* in the late 19th century, but by 1915 had been declared extinct because it had been overtaken by the more commercially viable Bourbon Red. In the 1940s there was a renewed interest in the breed and it was recreated from crosses of Black, Bourbon Red and Broad Breasted Bronze.

Originally called the Fawn or Chocolate in Britain, this light breed is now recognised here as the Buff. It is gingery brown with white wings, while the tail is edged with white. In the breed standards, more white than the edging on the tail feathers is regarded as a fault. The beak is horn coloured while the eyes are brown. Legs and feet are flesh coloured. Finished weights for the stag are 10 – 12.7kg. For a hen they are 5.4 – 8.2kg.

Bourbon Red

The Bourbon Red originated in Bourbon County, Kentucky in the late 19th century. The breeder was a Mr Barbee and he used crosses of the Buff, Bronze, and White Holland turkeys. They were originally called Bourbon Butternuts but were subsequently named Bourbon Reds.

The plumage is of a striking brownish red with thin black edgings to the male's feathers, although this latter feature is absent in the female's plumage. Both sexes have white flights, and white tail feathers with a reddish bar. The legs, feet and beak are horn coloured, while the eyes are light brown. The face, wattles and caruncles should be bright red. Under the standards, a pale ground colour or the presence of black flecks on the plumage are regarded as faults.

Although this is not primarily a commercial bird today, there are a number of breeders in the UK working to improve it, and there are some Bourbon Reds being sold at Christmas. The finished weights for a stag are 10 – 12.7kg, while those for a hen are 5.4 – 8.2kg.

Pied turkeys

Ronquieres

The Ronquieres is an old pied or black and white breed recorded in Belgium in the 16th century and is named after the district in which they were reared for the Brussels meat market. The breed almost died out early in the 20th century but it survived and is now kept going by breeders in Belgium, France and other areas of northern Europe. There are a number of varieties of the Ronquieres as follows:

Ermine: This has a yellow/fawn ground colour with fine black edging to the feathers.

Knefelder: This is a variety with partridge or fine pencilled plumage.

Tricoloré du Colorado: Similar to the Ronquieres in all other respects, this has yellowish shoulders.

Cröllwitzer

This is another of the so-called pied breeds that are primarily white or light coloured birds with black edging to a number of the feathers. Now standardised as a light breed in Britain, it was selectively bred in Germany from the Ronquieres in order to increase the finished weight.

The neck and the head are white, while the breast and back feathers are white edged with a black band with thin white outer strip. The flight and tail feathers are also white edged in black. The finished weights for a Cröllwitzer stag are 7.3 – 12.7kg, while for a hen they are 3.6 – 8.2kg.

Royal Palm

The Royal Palm is a small black and white pied breed that originated in Florida in the USA during the 1920s. It is essentially the same as the Cröllwitzer, although there are minor differences in the markings. It was first recognised as a standard breed in the USA in 1971. It was popular for a while because its white feathering produced a cleaner carcase without dark

Bronze hen. *(Katie Thear)*

feather stubs, but it was eventually ousted commercially by the Broad-Breasted White.

The Royal Palm is available in small numbers in Britain. There is also another variation called the Cornish Palm.

As referred to earlier, there are many other, often minor colour variations, to which the breeders may have given their own names and which are not recognised by any of the breed standards. Some may no longer be in existence. The same variation may also be given a different name, depending on the breeder and the locality. Some of the variations I have come across are:

Auburn	Charlevoix	Chestnut	Chocolate
Dark Brown	Light Brown	Nittany	Nutmeg,
Oregon Grey	Red	Silver Audubon	Tuscarora Red

Those selling turkeys for specific markets, such as the free-range or organic sectors, may also give different names to their own strains of existing pure breeds or hybrids. Some examples are:

Rustic Red
Wrolstad Bronze   Roly Poly Bronze Super Mini Bronze.
Super Mini White   RolyPoly White   Wrolstad Plumpie White

Wild Bush turkey. *(Kansas Information Office).*

Young Norfolk Blacks. *(Katie Thear)*

Bronze stag. (Katie Thear)

Crimson Dawn or Black-Winged Bronze stag and hen. (Katie Thear)

Brooder conditions are provided until the poults are hardy. *(Maywick)*

Six week old poults. After another couple of weeks they will be allowed outside. *(Katie Thear)*

Housing

Housing needs to provide shelter that is well insulated and free of draughts yet at the same time, well ventilated, if lung infections are to be avoided. It should be sufficiently roomy to cater for the appropriate number and size of birds, and also to exclude rats. The requirements vary, depending on the age of the birds, so it is appropriate to look at the options.

Brooder conditions

Day-old turkey poults are not large and can initially be reared in a fairly small area, but sufficient room must be allowed for their growth. For up to five weeks of age, plan for ten birds per square metre.

For growing birds after five weeks allow for 25kg weight of bird per square metre. In general terms this means no more than five growers per square metre and three finishers for the same area. If the birds are to be raised to organic standards, the *Soil Association* standards specify a maximum of two birds per square metre, with a minimum perch space per bird of 40cm.

Turkeys grow rapidly and they need enough space so that they do not become stressed by being too confined. This can cause problems that may be difficult to eradicate.

Their main requirements are protection from cold and damp weather, draughts and predators. One end of a rat-proof outhouse, barn or shed is suitable for setting up a brooding area. Make sure that the area and all the equipment are thoroughly cleaned and disinfected, particularly if chickens have been there beforehand. Ideally, chicken areas should be avoided because of the risk of disease transference. Chickens can pass on Blackhead disease which, while not affecting them, is a serious condition in turkeys.

After cleaning an area, let everything dry out properly before any birds are introduced. Young birds need warmth from a brooder lamp. These are available as electrically or propane gas-powered models. They should be in place and checked to ensure that the brooding area is warm enough before the birds arrive so that they are not subjected to a temperature drop 'shock' which will set them back.

The initial temperature at ground level for day olds should be 35°C. As they grow, they need progressively cooler temperatures. Gradually raising the lamp produces this effect. The best way of achieving the correct level at any given time, is to observe the behaviour of the poults. (See page 44).

  (Continued on Page 41)

Bourbon Red stag. *(Janice Houghton-Wallace. Turkey Club UK).*

Cröllwitzer stag and hen. *(Katie Thear)*

Buff stag. *(Norfolk Rare Breeds Centre).*

Royal Palm stag. *(Janice Houghton-Wallace. Turkey Club UK)*

Examples of Small-Scale Housing for Free-Range Turkeys

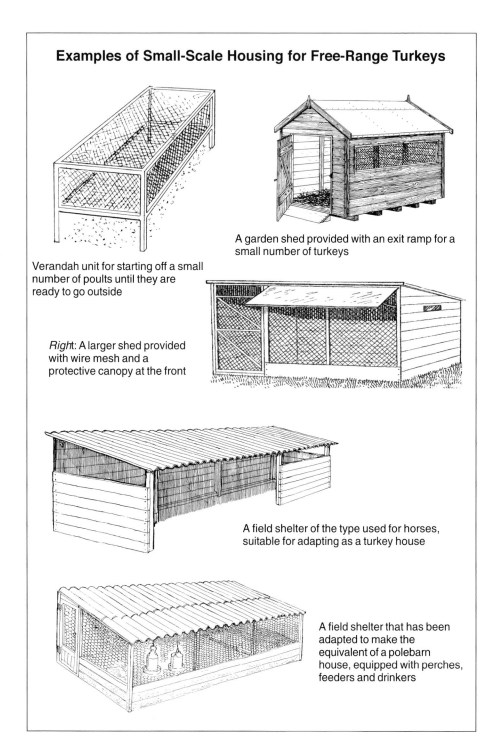

A garden shed provided with an exit ramp for a small number of turkeys

Verandah unit for starting off a small number of poults until they are ready to go outside

Right: A larger shed provided with wire mesh and a protective canopy at the front

A field shelter of the type used for horses, suitable for adapting as a turkey house

A field shelter that has been adapted to make the equivalent of a polebarn house, equipped with perches, feeders and drinkers

A well ventilated field shelter with perch adapted as housing for growing turkeys. *(Katie Thear)*

If they are staying huddled in a tight ball in the centre, under the lamp, they are too cold and it should be lowered.

If the poults are spread around the edges of the heated area, and avoiding the centre, they are too hot and the lamp should be raised.

If they are occupying the whole area, under the lamp and around the edges, they are contented.

The poults will need litter such as clean wood shavings on the floor to absorb droppings. Around 8cm deep will be sufficient.

It is a good idea to spread rough-textured paper over the litter for the first few days. This enables the poults to maintain their balance at a time when slipping and damaging the leg tendons is a possibility. It also stops them trying to eat the litter until they have become used to proper food.

(Continued on page 44)

Narrangansett stag. *(Janice Houghton-Wallace. Turkey Club UK).*

Lavender stag, a light version of the Blue/Slate. *(Katie Thear)*

Nebraskan hen. *(Rupert Stephenson)*

Blue/Slate stag. *(Janice Houghton-Wallace. Turkey Club UK).*

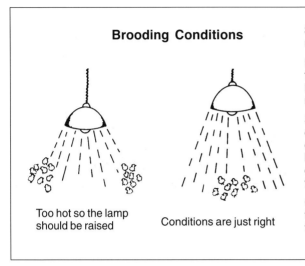

Brooding Conditions

Too hot so the lamp should be raised

Conditions are just right

Start at 35°C and gradually reduce slightly every day.

How the poults position themselves in relation to the lamp will indicate whether or not it is at the right height.

Sometimes poults need encouragement to eat and drink. Emulate the mother hen by dropping a few chick crumbs on paper to attract their attention.

Gently dip the beak in water, taking care not to get water in the nostrils.

Once the poults have found their feet and are eating properly, the paper can be removed. For a small number of poults, a piece of old blanket or towelling does equally well.

To confine the poults in the brooding area, they need to be surrounded by a low wall made up from wood or cardboard and about 60cm high. Brooder rings are available from suppliers or they can be constructed at home. They protect the birds from draughts as well as confining them to the warm area.

Food and drink should be available to the poults at all times. Depending on the number of birds, the drinkers may be automatically or manually re-filled, but if they are floor-standing ones, it is a good idea to place them on wire mesh so that any spilt water does not make wet patches in the litter. Such areas can become breeding grounds for pathogens such as coccidia.

A starter ration of turkey chick crumbs with floor containers placed on a piece of rough hardboard can be made available to them.

Initially a small building will be sufficient for the incoming poults, but a part of a larger building that will be their home as they grow may be more convenient. With a larger space, the birds can be moved easily onto fresh litter and the first area cleaned.

After four weeks the birds can be moved to their permanent quarters, although they should not be allowed outside before they are eight weeks in case they get a chill. A house for birds that are to have outside access does not have pop-holes but a normal door that opens outwards to make it easier for the large birds to go in and out. If it is fairly high off the ground, a ramp for ease of exit and entrance is recommended.

Free-range

Over the years there have been a number of ideas utilised for housing turkeys. What is appropriate will depend on the numbers being raised. Above all else, turkeys need light and fresh air and will thrive when allowed to graze on good quality pasture.

The grass must not have been used by chickens for several years, as parasites left by their droppings can prove fatal to turkeys. It should also be pasture that has not been used by turkeys the previous year. The birds need effective protection against foxes, either by having tall fences or by utilising electric fencing or netting.

The pasture needs to be dry and free of mud and poisonous plants. Within the grazing area the turkeys will appreciate windbreaks, a shady area and shelter from sudden showers, unless they are within easy access of their overnight house. The following are some of houses that are used for turkeys:

Verandah house

In the past, farmers with no pasture or barn space to spare often constructed verandahs specifically for the turkeys. This is a long structure with wire mesh along one or more sides. (See page 40). It is raised from the ground and has a slatted floor for the droppings to fall through. It really only works with a relatively small number of birds and is probably best used for the first few weeks when the young birds are more at risk from ground-based pathogens. Once well feathered and hardy, they can be released for free-ranging.

Fold unit

Fold units incorporating a housing area with an integral run similar to those used for chickens, have been used in the past, but they are a labour intensive solution as food and water have to be carried out to them regularly and they need to be moved every day onto fresh ground, a job that needs two people. Also each fold unit cannot hold more than a dozen large birds.

Straw bale house

A cheap solution if there is no field housing available is to build a house of straw bales. The bales can have wire netting around them on the outside to keep out predators and rodents, with a large mesh 'window' on one side to let in light and air. The roof can be made of corrugated iron sheets weighted down with rocks or bricks. The turkeys graze on the pasture on fine days within the protection of electric netting, and the straw bales can be composted at the end of the season. As with the fold units, food and water still need to be carried out to the field. Another disadvantage of this type of house is that, despite everything, rats and mice often do manage to find a way into the bales. Rodents raid the food supply as well as being carriers of disease.

(Continued on Page 49)

Head of Norfolk Black stag. *(Katie Thear)* Turkeys in Thuxton village sign

Bronze turkey poult. *(Wippell. 19th Century)* Turkey eggs. *(Kelly Turkey Farms)*

46

Commercial Broad-Breasted Bronze with outside straw bale perches. *(Kelly Turkey Farms).*

Day old Bronze chicks. *(Kelly Turkey Farms)*

Here, drinkers are placed outside the house to keep the floor litter dry. *(Katie Thear)*

A small turkey house equipped with perches and suspended feeders and drinkers. *(Katie Thea*

Pole barn

A good housing solution is to utilise and adapt a field shelter or large shed and provide access to the open air at appropriate times. Where there is no direct access to a field from the building, a straw yard can be made for the birds to walk in and out. (See Page 75).

A pole barn is in many respects ideal as it is open along one or more sides. The sides can be covered in mesh with the bottom 1.5 metres (4ft) boarded to prevent draughts. A field shelter can be adapted in the same way.

When young birds are transferred to a large barn area from a brooding pen, keep them confined to one end at first to help them adapt. Later as they have become used to the new environment, their floor space can be increased.

Polytunnel house

Some producers use dark plastic polytunnels with added insulation as housing for Christmas growers. There are specialist suppliers of these. It is important to ensure that the ventilation is adequate.

DIY house

A DIY turkey house can be constructed from available materials on the farm. We used to raise a couple of dozen turkeys each Christmas for our own use and to supply friends and neighbours. As our existing buildings were fully utilised, we constructed a turkey house in the field using spare wood and materials, and utilising the side of a hay barn as one of the walls. It did not look particularly attractive but it worked very well for a number of seasons and the turkeys went out to pasture on fine days. (See page 41).

Inside the house

Whatever its size, the house needs to have clean poultry wood shavings on the floor, not only to catch the droppings and provide a warm environment, but also to provide a scratching area if the birds are confined for any reason. Turkeys panic easily so it is best to rake and add to the existing litter when the birds are outside or have been confined to one side of the house. Raking the litter helps to aerate it and keep it dry and free of pathogens. Every effort should also be made to avoid damp areas in the litter.

Drinkers can be suspended or placed over a grating to take the run-off. Feeders can also be arranged in the same way.

On the question of panic, it is a good idea for the same person to do the daily feeding because the birds soon get used to him or her. Approaching the house or a group of turkeys should be done at a regular pace, with no sudden movements to startle them. They can easily damage their wing tips when they are inside, if they catch them against the walls or other structures.

Turkeys are perching birds so these should be made available to them in the house and outside. In the house, a minimum of 40cm perch space per

Keeping the Litter Dry

Drinkers should be suspended or placed in such a way that birds cannot gain access to damp areas

One way of ensuring that the floor litter does not get wet is to use a DIY solution such as this. *(Bulletin 67. MAFF. 1933)*

Perches

Perch space per bird - 40cm

Perch width - 8cm

Height from floor - 45cm maximum

Perches should be easily removed for cleaning.

An alternative to perches is to use straw bales.

bird is required. Straw bales make good perching areas and are at a suitable height for access. In fact, where wooden perches are used, they should be no higher than that of a straw bale (around 45cm) otherwise some heavy birds may find it difficult to get up onto them.

Flock and housing density

It is appropriate to mention that the number of turkeys housed together, or in an outside flock, should be kept relatively small, not only to minimise the possibility of disease transference, but also to reduce stress and the chances of injuries caused by panic and aggression. Reference was made earlier to the fact that hanging up objects such as unwanted CDs can provide a source of interest so that the birds are less likely to peck each other. Compressed seed balls do the same thing, as well as providing a feed supplement. Commercially, flock and housing densities allow for far greater numbers in a given space, but I personally would not recommend them. The following are the maximum number of birds required by organic standards. With the exception of *Soil Association* producers, most rearers follow the UK standards.

Soil Association Standards
House: 250
Range: 800 per hectare

Basic UK Standards
House: 2,500
1,000 per hectare

Feeding

With peacock and turkey, that nibbles off top,
are verie ill neighbors to seelie poore hop.
(Thomas Tusser. 1557)

The digestive system of the turkey is broadly the same as that of other poultry. Food is picked up by the pecking action of the beak and taken into the crop via the gullet. The crop is a temporary storage area where the food is softened by secretions from the mouth, gullet and the crop walls.

When the food is soft enough it moves into the glandular stomach where it is mixed with acidic gastric juices and and the enzyme pepsin which begin the process of breaking down the food. It then passes into the gizzard.

The gizzard has strong, muscular walls that grind up the food, particularly the grains, into a fine paste with the help of pieces of insoluble grit which have been taken in as 'grindstones'.

Together with water, the ground food then passes into the duodenum or the first looped part of the small intestine. Here, it is further subjected to secretions and enzymes from the pancreas, liver and gall bladder that continue to break the food down into its constituent parts. These are now ready for moving into the main section of the small intestine or ileum. Here, the nutrients are absorbed through the walls of the ileum into the blood capillaries, to be carried by the bloodstream to every part of the body.

Any remaining particles that cannot be absorbed, pass on to the colon or large intestine which is wider but much shorter than the small intestine. Here, any surplus liquid is extracted by projections known as caeca, although most of the water in the digestive system is filtered by the kidneys. The resultant urine is delivered by ureter tubes, to join the waste matter at the rectum. From here, both are expelled at the cloacal opening of the vent as faeces or droppings. The whitish part of the droppings is the urine.

Nutritional requirements

For the turkey to get the maximum benefit from its food intake it needs to have a properly balanced diet for each stage of growth, as well as access to constant supplies of fresh water and insoluble grit. The various food components are as follows:

Proteins

These are the main body builders that are responsible for growth and the maintenance of body tissues. They are made up of various constituents called amino acids and there are around a dozen of them. Some can be synthesised

If turkeys are fed outside it is advisable to use heavy based feeders that cannot be overturned. The feeding area should also be protected to exclude wild birds. *(Katie Thear)*

Outdoor turkeys using an automatic feeder for pellets or grain. The height can be adjusted, depending on the size of the birds. *(Hengrave Feeders)*

Digestive System

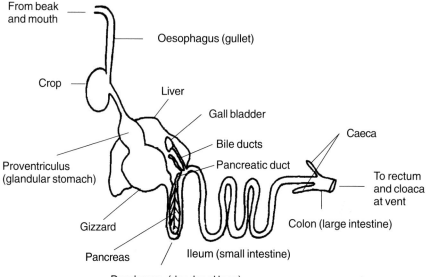

from other food constituents, while others must be taken in directly every day. This is one of the reasons why a balanced ration is essential; it is easy to give too much of one thing at the expense of another.

Proteins are found in animal and plant sources, but many of the free-range and organic proprietary rations are based on plant-sourced proteins.

Protein Sources

Animal Fishmeal, Milk products,
Invertebrates and small vertebrates from pasture ranging.

Plant Soya, Peas, Beans, Barley, Maize, Sunflowers, Oats, Wheat,
Clover, Grass, Lucerne, Dried Yeast, Potatoes, Linseed.

Energy foods

These are the food constituents that are needed to meet the normal body demands in relation to moving, breathing and anything else associated with being alive. Carbohydrates and oils are the main sources and a food's energy potential is called its ME (metabolisable energy) factor. This is measured in terms of megajoules per kilogram (MJ/kg). Carbohydrates are also the main source of fibre; the latter being essential in the diet to prevent upsets.

Energy and Fibre Sources

Wheat, Barley, Triticale, Maize, Oats, Millet, Soya, Sunflowers, Linseed, Molasses, Bran.

Minerals

Minerals are inorganic substances that are required in small quantities to maintain health and to guard against deficiency diseases. Some are needed in such tiny quantities that they are referred to as *trace elements*. Minerals are usually added to proprietary rations, but free-ranging birds will also acquire a certain proportion from the ground or from pasture plants.

Natural Mineral Sources

Calcium	Lucerne, Green vegetables, Calcified seaweed, Milk products, Molasses, Dried Yeast, Soil (if land is chalky)
Cobalt	Calcified seaweed
Copper	Cereals, Beans, Soil (in some local soils)
Iodine	Calcified seaweed, Washed seaweed
Iron	Nettles, Chicory, Parsley, Dandelions, Chickweed
Magnesium	Oats, Beans, Soya, Grass, Spinach
Manganese	Lucerne, Wheat, Maize, Millet, Oats, Molasses, Dried yeast
Phosphorus	Lucerne, Grass, Oats, Dandelions, Calcified seaweed
Potassium	Lucerne, Maize, Wheat, Soya, Sunflowers, Potato, Yeast, Molasses
Selenium	Green vegetables, Lucerne, Maize, Yeast
Sodium	Grass, Lucerne, Maize, Molasses, Yeast, Sunflowers
Zinc	Lucerne, Soya, Molasses, Wheat, Maize, Sunflowers, Yeast

Vitamins

These are organic compounds that are essential for the maintenance of health. They are usually added to proprietary feeds, but the birds will also take in a certain amount through their free-ranging activities.

Natural Vitamin Sources

Vitamin A	Grass, Maize, Kale and other brassicas, Carrots, Nettles
B1 (Thiamine)	Most cereals
B2 (Riboflavin)	Grass, Soya, Dried yeast
B3 (Niacin)	Wheat and other cereals
B5 (Pantothenic acid)	Grass, Comfrey, Yeast, Molasses
B6 (Pyridoxine)	Soya, Wheat, Yeast
B12 (Cobalmin)	Comfrey, Calcified seaweed
D3	Sunshine, Wheat, Maize and other cereals
E	Grass, Wheat, Maize, Kale and other brassicas
H (Biotin)	Maize, Lucerne, Grass
K	Lucerne, Grass

Proprietary feeds

There is more than one way to organise feed for turkeys. You can make up your own balanced rations from available cereals and pulses and add the necessary minerals and vitamins. However, the work has already been done by the feed compounders who supply perfectly balanced feeds either in the form of pellets or as coarse ground meal. Either of these is suitable for there is little or no waste, and by following the supplier's instructions, healthy birds can be reared and grown to their optimum weights. There are several proprietary feeds available in the following forms:

Starter crumbs
These are for the young birds. They are high in protein, around 28% for most commercial turkeys, but around 23% for the slower-growing traditional breeds that are being raised organically.

Starter crumbs are normally fed from hatch until around six weeks of age. They are available with or without a coccidiostat to protect against coccidiosis.

Grower's ration
Starter crumbs are followed by a grower's ration that can be fed up to 12 - 16 weeks. They have a protein content of around 21%. As with any change in diet, it is a good idea to introduce a change of feed gradually so that there is less likelihood of a digestive upset. For example, introduce a little grower's ration to the starter crumbs and gradually reduce the latter while increasing the former.

Finisher ration
A finisher ration with a further reduced protein content can be fed next, until slaughtering time. When raising a small number of birds some people dispense with the finisher ration and just continue with the grower's feed.

Breeder ration
If birds are not being raised for meat but are destined to become part of a breeding flock, they can transfer to a poultry breeder's ration after 12 weeks of age. This is specially formulated for breeding poultry and has a high energy and protein content (around 19%). It ensures that the progeny of the breeding birds are not affected by any nutritional deficiencies in the parents.

Variation in proprietary feeds
As referred to earlier, the balance of oils, protein, fibre and minerals in the feed (the latter shown as ash) changes as the turkeys grow. This balance also varies a little in the feeds from different feed suppliers, with some being produced for the large, quick-growing turkey sector, while others are aimed at slower growing, organic turkeys. Here is an example:

Typical Organic Rations

Starter	Grower	Finisher
Oil: 6.2%	Oil: 4.9%	Oil: 3.9%
Protein: 23.3%	Protein: 21.3%	Protein: 15.5%
Fibre: 4.3%	Fibre: 3.8%	Fibre: 3.9%
Ash: 7.1%	Ash: 6.2%	Ash: 4.9%

Feeding grain

Feeding a whole grain ration has several advantages. It is popular with the birds and there is some evidence that there is less likelihood of aggression problems where it is given.

Grain can also be used to balance the proprietary feed if the turkeys are growing too rapidly. For example, the amount of proprietary pellets can be reduced and just given in the morning, while grain such as wheat is given in the afternoon. Insoluble poultry grit should be available at all times, where the birds can help themselves as necessary.

Storing feeds

All feedstuffs must be stored so that they do not become damp and they are secure from vermin. Mouldy food or that contaminated by rodents can cause disease. Screw-top plastic dustbins are good, but hungry rats can gnaw through them, so if in doubt use metal containers.

The nutritional value of feeds also reduces over time, so do not buy and store feed for a long time. It is better to buy little and often so that the birds always have freshly milled rations, although this is obviously more expensive than buying in bulk.

Feeding practice

The best method of providing feed and water under cover is with the use of suspended cylindrical feeders and drinkers set at the height of the bird's back. This will avoid a need to reach down with more risk of spillage.

Do not put too much feed in at one time, and ensure that the manufacturer's instructions are followed. Provide enough containers so that the birds are not pushing to get to them and spilling the food. As a general guide, there should be at least 5cm of linear trough space per poult for the first couple of weeks, increasing to 10cm by six weeks. Older growers and adults need at least 20cm. The feeders and drinkers will need to be raised regularly as the birds grow and this is an opportunity to scrub them out to maintain necessary hygienic conditions. If you are raising quite a number of birds, you will need to provide extra feeders and drinkers as they grow to make sure that they continue to have easy access. In these circumstances, water can be provided automatically to suspended drinkers.

Grit should also be made available in a robust container which cannot be tipped over, so that the birds can help themselves whenever necessary.

In winter conditions, check regularly that the water supply is not frozen. Barn raised turkeys can become bored and bad tempered, so bunches of cabbage and lettuce leaves can be suspended which will help to keep them interested and occupied. Reference has already been made to the success of using suspended CDs in this way. (See page 16).

Turkeys can also be nervous and excitable so when entering the barn and seeing to the feeders and drinkers, move slowly and speak quietly so as not to frighten them. In time they will become used to the one who feeds them.

Amount of food

The amount of food consumed will depend on a number of factors, including the breed, the strain, age, the weather, the environment and the availability of supplementary foods on range. As a general guide, the following amounts of proprietary feeds will be consumed during the season, but it is emphasised again that this is only a generalisation:

Average amount consumed
1.8kg per poult of crumbs
8kg per bird of grower rations
15kg per bird of finisher rations

It was said earlier that commercial strains of slow-growing turkeys for the free-range and organic sectors are available in a range of finished weights. Knowing what these are helps in future planning.

Performance Data for Different Strains of Commercial Bronze Turkeys

	Super Mini Bronze	Roly Poly Bronze	Wrolstad Bronze
20 weeks	5.9kg - 9.37kg *	6.28kg - 9.87kg	6.59kg - 10.36kg
22 weeks	6.32kg - 10.10kg	7.16kg - 10.65kg	8.00kg - 11.20kg
24 weeks	6.64kg - 10.90kg	7.47kg - 11.65kg	8.30kg - 12.49kg

(Ref: Kelly Turkey Farms)   * Hen and Stag

Feeding on range

Turkeys will benefit from access to fresh pasture and can be turned out as soon as they are fully feathered, as long as the weather is fine and adequate shelters are provided. If they find plenty of food there amongst the soil and the pasture plants and grasses, compound feeds can be reduced, which is a worthwhile financial saving. Do not allow turkeys onto land or ground that is wet as this can harbour coccidiosis protozoans.

In addition to outside shelters for the birds, feeders, drinkers and grit containers should also have shaded protection where wild birds cannot gain access. On range the turkeys may not use the grit containers if they are able to pick up enough small stones from the ground.

Perimeter Fencing to Deter Foxes

Wing Clipping

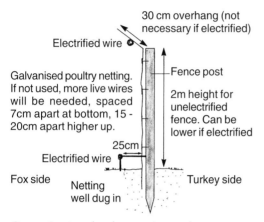

30 cm overhang (not necessary if electrified)

Electrified wire

Galvanised poultry netting. If not used, more live wires will be needed, spaced 7cm apart at bottom, 15 - 20cm apart higher up.

Fence post

2m height for unelectrified fence. Can be lower if electrified

25cm

Electrified wire

Fox side

Netting well dug in

Turkey side

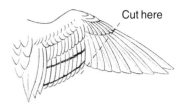

Cut here

Only the primary feathers on one wing are trimmed, if it is necessary to confine particularly flighty birds.

It is better to rely on high fences, for although painless, and the feathers will grow again, it is unsightly.

Organic standards require turkeys to spend at least a third of their lives outside. Grain or wheat can be provided on the pasture in a feeder or scattered on the grass, and the proportion of grain in the diet can be increased if the turkeys are growing too quickly, as referred to earlier.

It is important not to put down too much grain, as any left behind will attract rodents. In hot summer weather the birds will consume more water so shade provision and regular checks are essential. A bucket placed in a tyre makes a stable drinker and is easy to refill. On a larger scale a field tank with an automatic refill will be suitable.

Turkeys forage well on good quality pasture that has not been used beforehand by chickens. Turkeys are vulnerable to blackhead disease that can be picked up if they graze over land where chickens have been. Proprietary feeds will normally include an antibiotic coccidiostat to protect the turkeys from this danger, but it is possible to purchase turkey rations that are free of this medication. Organic turkey rations do not contain a coccidiostat. Our own turkey grazing area was compromised one year by a number of chickens wandering in through gaps in the hedge from a neighbour's flock.

If a bird needs antibiotic or other veterinary treatment, then this is, of course, allowed under organic standards. It is their routine use where there is no health necessity that is banned. After necessary medication has ceased there is a withdrawal period during which time treated birds cannot be sold. This varies, according to the standards, as follows:

UK Organic Standards	Soil Association Organic Standards
28 days	56 days

Predator protection on range

No matter how big turkeys grow, they are always vulnerable to foxes that can do a great deal of damage if they are ever able to get amongst them.

A large turkey house with ventilation on both sides. *(Brian Hale)*

Ensure that the flock returns from the pasture each day before dusk to the safety of their secure house.

Even with a secure house, foxes can come earlier in the day so sturdy perimeter fencing is essential. This can either be wire netting that is at least 2m (6.5ft) high and well dug in, or electric fencing. (See opposite).

Turkeys can also be regulated on range by the use of moveable electric poultry netting so that they have access to new areas as the first show signs of wear. As they are flock birds like ducks and geese, turkeys are easy to move from one place to another, although they can be extremely voluble.

Home mixed rations

If you are in a place where turkey rations are not readily available, it is possible to manage without them. The poults can be started with chick crumbs (without any antibiotics if preferred), then a home made grower's ration can be made up as follows:

Home Made Ration

1 part bran, 2 parts maize meal or oats, 1 part soya extract and 2 parts wheat.

This can be fed two or three times a day together with insoluble poultry grit to enable them to break down their feed properly.

When we kept dairy animals, we always fed our Christmas turkeys with coarse barley meal mixed with surplus goat's milk or skimmed cow's milk. This was fed twice a day with a separate afternoon feed of either mixed grain, or wheat. The latter is cheaper. Barley meal produces a bird with a more golden skin and flesh, by comparison with most white birds.

Breeding Saddle

It protects the hen's sides without restricting her wings. The stag's claws should also be clipped.

Breeding Pens

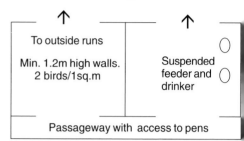

To outside runs

Min. 1.2m high walls.
2 birds/1sq.m

Suspended
feeder and
drinker

Passageway with access to pens

Lighting can be provided in indoor breeding pens early in the season to induce earlier egg laying.

Loss of Water during Incubation

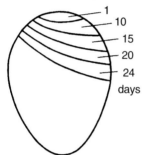

1
10
15
20
24
days

The size of the air space during incubation is an indication of whether the correct amount of water is being lost, relative to the number of days as shown above.

Fertile Egg

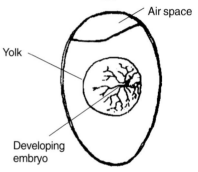

Air space

Yolk

Developing
embryo

Candling an egg by viewing it against a bright light enables checks to be made as to its fertility and development.

Humidity and Temperature Requirements for Turkey Eggs

Incubation
Day 1 - 24: 55%

Hatching
Day 25 - 28: 75%

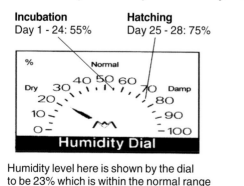

Humidity level here is shown by the dial to be 23% which is within the normal range for a room in which the incubator is housed

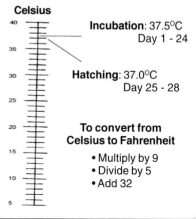

Celsius

Incubation: 37.5°C
Day 1 - 24

Hatching: 37.0°C
Day 25 - 28

**To convert from
Celsius to Fahrenheit**

• Multiply by 9
• Divide by 5
• Add 32

Breeding

When they get their head feathers, they are hardy enough.
(Cottage Economy. William Cobbett. 1821)

There are three ways in which turkeys are kept on a small scale. Some of these will involve breeding on-site. The turkey enterprises may be differentiated as follows:

• Farmers and smallholders who buy in poults during the summer to rear for the Christmas market.

• Breeders who raise their own turkeys for the market and sell the surplus poults.

• Enthusiasts who keep and breed traditional coloured turkey breeds for interest and showing.

As referred to earlier, turkeys can be classified by their breeds or plumage colour, and by their type, as there are within some breeds, large, medium and small birds that finish at different weights.

Genetic factors

Plumage colour, body conformation, breast width and egg production are genetic factors that pass from one generation to another. Both body conformation and egg size are of good heritability and can be improved with selected breeding. Egg production and hatchability are of low heritability so these factors can only be improved over time with family breeding and individual selection.

Some plumage colours are dominant and others recessive. For example, black turkeys mated with bronze produce black offspring. If these offspring are then mated together, their offspring will be either black or bronze.

Although black plumage is dominant to bronze, the latter is dominant to any plumage colour other than black. So, if bronze turkeys are mated with another colour their progeny will all be bronze. If these are then mated with each other their offspring will, as before, produce both bronze birds and those of the original colour. If these latter, original colour progeny are mated together they will breed true. This plumage colour is recessive to bronze. These colour factors can be summed up as follows:

Black x Bronze = Black

Blacks (from Black/ Bronze) x Blacks (from Black/Bronze) = Black or Bronze

Bronze x Any Other Colour = Bronze

Bronze (from Bronze/AOC) x Bronze (from Bronze/AOC) = Bronze or Original Colour

Original Colour x Original Colour = Original Colour

Breeding stock

Those keeping coloured turkeys as a hobby may be interested in having several different breeds. In this situation, buying top quality birds at the outset is essential, for the capacity to improve the quality of the stock is limited by the small numbers kept of each breed. Real improvements in fertility, egg production and hatchability can only be achieved through detailed record keeping based on a system of trap nesting. This is a very time consuming process and is unlikely to be practical for small breeders.

Selection

The careful selection of both stags and hens is the secret of producing good quality breeding birds. The first step is to acquire good quality stock. When buying birds find out about food conversion, body conformation, meat to bone ratio and their finished weight range. For breeding stock, ask about their fertility, hatchability, egg production and weights at maturity. Check each bird carefully to ensure that it is well fleshed and free of deformities, old wounds or external parasites. Turkeys are meat birds so good conformation and meat to bone ratio is important, but excessive weight is to be avoided.

Before you buy, make sure that you know what you are looking for. This means finding out about the breed and its characteristics beforehand. Birds that are being bred for showing may have been selected for different characteristics, such as carriage, appearance and feather colouring, rather than for more utilitarian considerations. Traditionally, the best breeding birds were those that were fairly upright and not too broad and heavy in the breast because this can lead to difficulty in mating.

Even with some of the traditional heavy breeds, there is a danger in breeding for excessive backward curve of the neck and too large a breast. As with most things, moderation is best, with ideal breeders having the following:

Good Breeder Characteristics

- **Healthy and vigorous**: no weaknesses and tendency to illness
- **Reasonably upright in carriage**: weight evenly distributed to walk well
- **Good meat to bone ratio**: for a table bird, without being excessive
- **Good example of breed standard**: not at expense of utility factors
- **Able to mate naturally**: A.I. is not appropriate for traditional breeds
- **Good egg production**: hens lay an acceptable number of quality eggs
- **Good fertility**: acceptable number of fertile eggs
- **Good hatchability**: acceptable number of eggs that hatch

Rearing good stock

If rearing your own potential breeding stock, look for a uniformity of size, shape and colouring, and only keep the best for breeding on. Maintain detailed records so that you know which are the healthy, vigorous birds with good production.

Tag or ring the birds that are kept, with details of their parentage. Change stags regularly to avoid inbreeding. Hen birds producing poor quality poults should be removed from the breeding programme. Maintaining these standards and separating and culling sub-standard birds will lead to better stock to sell to customers.

To achieve these goals effectively, quite a number of birds may need to be kept. The greater the number, the greater the opportunity to improve the quality of the stock from one season to the next. Therefore, for the smallholder or small-scale breeder hoping to produce good birds to sell on, there is a case for concentrating at the outset on just one breed, such as bronze or black turkeys where there is likely to be a ready market.

Breeder management

Both stags and hens should have identification tags or rings so that accurate records can be kept for each of the birds. They are available from specialist suppliers. A breeding ratio of one stag to ten hens is the right proportion. Fewer hens may lower the overall fertility. Conversely, having too many hens will produce the same effect. This is a generalisation, for there can be considerable variation, with heavier breeds often having a lower ratio.

Turkeys start to lay eggs from 28 - 30 weeks onwards. They lay most eggs in their first year, with numbers decreasing in the second year and again in their third year. Stags are also at their most fertile in their first year so using young birds to produce poults for sale gives the best results. A stag used for a second season will have a reduced fertility. Balanced against this, is the fact that performance will be a known quantity from the second year, if accurate records have been kept.

It is a good idea to keep some stags in reserve in case one is needed. Reserve stags should be penned out of sight of the breeding flock to prevent over-excitability. If a stag is inactive or if the eggs produced after his mating activity are not fertile, he will need to be replaced.

Introducing the sexes

Introduce the sexes about a month before laying begins. This is the time to change the diet over to breeders' pellets, if they are not already on it. It will ensure that there are no deficiency diseases to be passed on to the progeny.

Provide them with a good quality ration and fresh water with access to insoluble poultry grit at all times. Once breeding begins, rotate stags each week, returning the removed one to a pen by himself. Careful checking of egg fertility should soon show whether a stag is worth using or not. Bear in mind that fertility and hatchability are not the same thing. Fertility is indicated by whether an egg is fertile when candled over a bright light. Hatchability is whether it eventually hatches. Both are expressed as percentages, with the higher ones being indicative of good breeding stock.

A breeding flock does not have to be kept inside. They can be out in a protected yard or on pasture during the day and are much better for being so. Place their feed in an area to which wild birds do not have access. Covered feeders with an enclosed unit from where the turkeys can trigger a small amount of feed at a time are suitable. Water containers need to be raised above the ground on a plinth, to keep contamination to a minimum.

Mating

Depending on the scale of the enterprise, either a system of flock mating or of pen mating will be used.

Flock mating

With a big breeding flock, flock mating can be practised. This is where a large area of ground is available so that several stags can be run with the females. It should be emphasised that it is only a practical proposition on a field scale, where the space is sufficient to allow the stags to form their own breeding sets, without the risk of fighting. On a smaller scale, pen mating is more appropriate and more accurate records can be kept.

Pen mating

An indoor or barn pen used for mating should have plenty of light and ventilation or be near to the open air as the turkeys need these conditions. Fertility is also directly affected by the amount of light.

The pens need to be at least 1.2m high. If the birds are particularly flighty, or have not had one wing clipped, it may be necessary to increase the height to 1.8m. If two pens are adjacent, the first 90cm should be of solid material to prevent stags from each pen trying to fight. It is a good idea to have two pens and alternate the birds each month to provide an opportunity to clean one out and give that area a rest. The floor of the breeding pen should be wood shavings or clean chopped straw.

Perches or straw bales should be no higher than 45cm from the ground. Nest boxes can be placed along the shadiest side of the pen. A nest box should be at least 45cm x 45cm x 60cm high. As well as individual nest boxes, you could provide larger communal nest boxes because turkeys will accept them and they may be better able to spread themselves out. Nests should be accessible for egg collecting without needing to enter the pen. It is also a good idea to place drinkers and feeders where they can be removed for cleaning and refilling without having to enter the pen.

Hen protection

Stags mounting turkey hens can cause damage with their claws, tearing the skin of the hen and causing nasty wounds, although this is more likely to occur with the heavier breeds. For protection, the hen can be fitted with a canvas mating saddle. This fits over her back and sides without restricting her wings. The stag should also have his claws clipped and spurs filed. The

A newy-hatched Bronze turkey poult. *(Brian Hale)*

protective process continues throughout the egg laying period, with each successful mating fertilising 10 to 12 eggs.

Artificial insemination

As referred to earlier, large commercial breeds may not be able to mate normally, so artificial insemination will be needed, although it is not advised for the small scale breeder of traditional breeds. Semen can be collected from the stag two to three times a week and transferred to the hens within half an hour as it degrades quickly. One insemination will remain effective for two weeks. It is emphasised that the technique should only be attempted by those who have undertaken a practical course in the procedure.

Eggs

Collect eggs twice a day and keep records of sizes, frequency, and the number of good poults produced from each pen in a season. Lighter breeds can lay up to 100 eggs in a season and come into lay earlier, whereas the heavier types may lay as few as 50, with the laying season lasting from 16 to 20 weeks. Laying begins at around 28 weeks onwards, depending on the breed.

Turkeys normally lay between April and June although there may be some eggs laid in March and July, with the earliest eggs producing the heaviest birds at Christmas. Providing artificial light early in the season may be needed as laying birds need about fourteen hours of light per day. It need not be much extra light, and a low wattage bulb over a pen is sufficient. It should have a timer so that the amount of light can be programmed, unless it is a digital system that calculates the amount of light automatically and compensates accordingly.

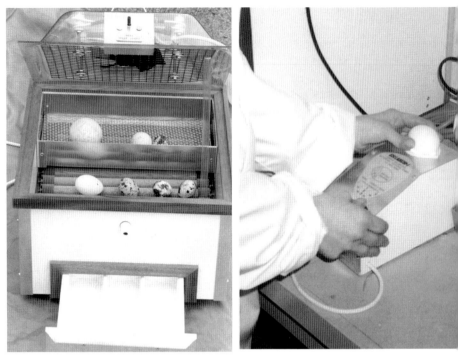

An example of a small, fully-automatic incubator, here shown with a variety of eggs. The turkey egg is top left. (Only similar eggs should be incubated at the same time). *(Curfew)*

Candling an egg against a bright light. *(Katie Thear)*

Start with lighting at the beginning of February, adding an extra hour each week so that there is a total of fourteen hours (artificial + natural) by early March. In a good year, a breeding pen of ten layers should produce more than 500 eggs. If you hatch more than you need, the surplus can be sold as poults, although it makes sense to sell to those outside the immediate area, who might otherwise end up as competitors. This will add to the profitability of the enterprise.

Monitoring Breeding Peformance				
Pen No.	Eggs set per hen	Fertility %	Hatchability % fertile eggs	Total No. Poults

To calculate fertility %
Number of eggs in incubator = a
Number fertile at candling = b
% of fertile eggs = $\dfrac{b \times 100}{a}$

To calculate hatchability %
Number of fertile eggs = b
Number of eggs hatched = c
% of fertile eggs hatched = $\dfrac{c \times 100}{b}$

Incubation

Fertile eggs can be incubated naturally by the bird or artificially using a purpose-made incubator.

Broodiness

As with chickens, turkey hens can go broody. They do not make particularly good mothers, although there are always exceptions. On the whole, it is better to use an incubator for incubating and hatching the eggs.

A broody turkey will take over a nest box and refuse to budge, complaining when anyone tries to move her. If broodiness is not required, the best thing is to remove her to a small, cool coop within sight of the breeding pen. She can stay there with food and water until the broodiness has gone. This could take a week or two. When she is no longer broody return her to active service in the breeding pen.

Artificial incubation

Store the eggs for the incubator in a cool pantry, broad end up in cartons for no more than a week before incubating them. Allow them to get to room temperature before introducing them into the machine and dip them in an egg sanitant to help ensure that they are free of pathogens. Turkey eggs are equivalent in size to duck eggs.

The longer eggs are kept before incubation, the lower the rate of hatchability, with the reduction amounting to around 2% per day after lay. Every egg should be clean, free from cracks or other surface damage and not misshapen. The incubator must also be clean, disinfected and already running at the required temperature before introducing the eggs. It should be set up in a place where there is very little outside variation in temperature. A spare room in the house or a specially insulated area of a shed will suffice.

An automatic incubator will maintain the correct temperature and humidity and also turn the eggs regularly. Ensure that the manufacturer's instructions are followed for there are slight variations with different models.

The optimum temperature at the centre of the egg is 37.5°C, with a humidity level of 55% for the incubation period.

After a week remove the eggs one by one and candle them. (See opposite and Page 60). This will show up those eggs that are not fertile and will also reveal whether the humidity level is correct from the size of the air sac. Discard the infertile eggs, returning the others immediately.

Around day 25 the eggs will begin to pip and the temperature should be reduced to 37.0°C , with the humidity increased to 75%. The eggs should hatch by day 28. Once dry, fluffed up and active, the newly hatched poults will need warmth, chick crumbs and water in a place protected from rats. (See Page 36). For a comprehensive coverage of incubation, see *Incubation: A Guide to Hatching and Rearing*.

Christmas Turkeys

We bought all the commercial bronze turkeys in the country and made our own breed. (Paul Kelly. Kelly Turkey Farms)

Small-scale producers of turkeys for Christmas are not in competition with large commercial producers. Instead they are catering for the growing market in freshly killed turkeys that have been reared on a non-intensive basis. Many people today are wary of all forms of intensively produced meat and demand a good quality bird for their Christmas table, so smallholders who have raised their birds humanely with good quality food are ideally placed to meet public aspirations.

Know your market

Before ordering any poults, it is essential to have a clear idea of the potential market, and to be able to answer the following questions:

- What breed should be chosen: commercial or traditional?
- How many should be raised?
- At what finished weight range?
- What proportion will be sold directly to customers?
- What outlets will take the remainder?
- At what prices will they be sold?
- Is my site suitable for farm gate sales?
- Can I meet the relevant regulations?
- To what standard will they be raised: free-range or organic?

Of course, it is impossible to be precise about these estimates of the market but it is important to try. Look at the competition. How many turkeys are being sold at the farm gate in your locality, and to what standard? Will they be free-range or organic, bearing in mind that these are legal terms and cannot be used without adherence to the necessary standards?

Talk to local restaurants, hotels, and to local consumer groups, together with organisations such as Women's Institutes and environmental bodies to see what kind of birds people are interested in buying.

See whether they are already buying local farm turkeys, what they are looking for and what they are prepared to pay. Prices are crucial both for customer acceptance and for profits.

Is there a shortage of supply of any kind? Perhaps there is for organically raised turkeys. A great deal can be learned by asking the right questions. Finally, when starting out do not be too ambitious. Use the first season to gain practical experience, and do not raise more birds than you are confident you can sell. After that, the business can be developed in future years.

A clear sign showing if the site is open is essential. *(Katie Thear)*

Sales and Marketing

Generating sales

Base your plans on the market research results. Is there already a glut of good quality local turkeys in your locality? If so, maybe you should be doing something else! Assuming that you plan to go ahead, decide exactly what you are going to do and go for it! Your turkeys will not sell themselves so vigorous promotion is essential, particularly as you are unknown.

Prepare a range of posters, signs, press releases and leaflets and get them out at the beginning of October to encourage customers to give you advance orders. Try to be imaginative and give your enterprise an attractive and easily remembered name.

Emphasise the positive qualities of your birds, particularly if there are any unique features for the area, such as the availability of a traditional breed or organically-reared turkeys. Local papers, television and radio stations need good stories so tell them what you are up to, and why. For the local press make sure there is a good picture for them, perhaps of you with one of your 'special quality birds'.

Getting the finished weight right

Advance orders from customers will indicate their weight requirements. Bringing the birds to slaughter at the right weights takes experience. Customers know that it is not easy to be precise in these matters but they will be unhappy with birds that are radically different in weight from their stated requirements. Few will wish to have a turkey that is too big for the oven!

Monitoring weights				Sample weighing of a few
Date	Weight	Feed Consumed	F.C.R.	birds can be done to produce average for batch.
				Feed Conversion Ratio is amount of food eaten in relation to weight gain.

If the whole flock finishes up overweight, this also represents wasted feed costs. Try to monitor the weights of the birds as they grow, in order to get it right, and to check that the feed conversion ratio is reasonable. The difference in weight between a live bird and an oven ready carcase is about 18 - 25%, so a turkey slaughtered at around 12kg will weigh around 9.5kg to the customer. To avoid problems, consider the following:

• Choose a traditional, slow-growing breed.
• Ensure that they have plenty of outdoor exercise.
• Buy the right mix of males and females. Poults are available as 'AH' (as hatched) or sexed, which will be more expensive, but females will be smaller.
• If they are showing signs of excessive growth, reduce the proprietary feed and make up the deficit with wheat.

Slaughter

If there is a local abattoir, it may be appropriate to use their facilities, but the turkeys will have to be delivered there and the carcases collected. It is far better to slaughter birds on site so they are spared the stress of travelling.

For on-site slaughtering it is necessary to register beforehand with the local *Environmental Health Department*. The *Welfare of Animals (Slaughter and Killing) Regulations 1995*, specify the humane considerations to be followed. The *Humane Slaughter Association* has a publication entitled *Practical Slaughter of Poultry* which is essential reading. If an electric stunner is used, a license will be required, but not if the birds are killed by neck dislocation. There is a lot of work involved so some experienced help will be needed. Again, it will need to have been considered before embarking on the project.

Some training or practical experience is strongly recommended before undertaking on-farm slaughtering and no one should attempt it unless they are fully confident in being able to do it quickly, efficiently and humanely.

Before slaughter, try to keep the birds calm and unstressed. Withdraw food about 12 hours beforehand but make sure that the birds continue to have fresh water. After slaughter, cut the jugular vein of the neck in order to drain the blood into a container before the carcases are hung in a cool room.

If there are insufficient direct customer orders, some birds can be sent to butchers as 'Long-Legged' birds. This is where the birds are killed and plucked but not eviscerated. The turkeys should be entire, including the head and feet and every bird must be labelled with the supplier's details.

Flow Chart for Processing Turkeys

To cool room, rough-plucked and hung until delivered to butchers if 'long-legged'. ← **Turkeys killed** ← Withdraw food for 12 hours but access to water. No stress.

⬇

To cool room for hanging until evisceration ← **Plucking** → Feathers disposed

(Environmental Health Office will advise on disposal of waste)

⬇

To cool room until dressed and packaged ← **Eviscerating** → Blood and viscera disposed

⬇

To cool room until collected by customers ← **Dressing, packaging and labelling**

Jugular veins

Bleeding after slaughter

Plucking

Plucking should be undertaken straight away, while the carcases are still warm. Aim to make this process as quick as possible, removing the wing and tail feathers first, followed by those of the back and the rest. There are sometimes experienced pluckers in country areas. If doing it yourself, practical training is essential. It is not difficult to find someone to demonstrate.

Wear an overall and work in light airy conditions. After dry plucking, the stub feathers can be singed off with a small, gas-powered torch that is available for the purpose. There are also small machine pluckers available.

Alternatively, it may be worth looking into the question of wax plucking. This is where the carcase is dipped into a hot wax solution, left to cool and when the wax is removed, it takes all the feathers with it. There are specialist suppliers of slaughtering, plucking and dressing equipment.

After plucking, the birds can be hung in a cold room for 4 - 10 days in order to tenderise and flavour the meat.

Evisceration

This involves cutting off the head and feet, and removing the viscera from each bird. During evisceration and dressing the carcases should be kept at no more than 4°C so it is vital to have a cool working area in addition to a cool store. Attention to hygiene at all stages is paramount. The technique is best acquired by demonstration for it is important to produce carcases that look professional. The *Environmental Health Department* will advise on all these matters and on the best method of blood, feather and viscera disposal.

Dressing

Again, the process of producing a professionally dressed carcase is best learned at a course or by having it demonstrated by an experienced person. It involves removing the strong leg tendons. (Tendon removers are available from suppliers). The heart, neck and cleaned-out gizzard can be placed in a small plastic bag to be sold along with the carcase, for many people like to use them to make gravy. The best meat birds have a pronounced 'dimple' separating the two areas of the breast.

Packaging and labelling

As the turkeys are finished, place each one in a clear plastic bag with a label. This should include the following information:

- Your name and address.
- The product description, eg, organically raised turkey.
- Advice on storage conditions, eg, keep chilled at 4°C or less.
- The use by date, eg, 7 days if supplying before Christmas.
- The certification code if the bird has been organically raised.
- The finished weight.
- The customer's name.

Ready printed labels can be organised through a specialist company such as *Danro*, or plain ones with typed or hand-written details can be used.

Dealing with customers

Having been successful in attracting customers, you will want to ensure that they come back again. Their experience of visiting the site should therefore be pleasant and convenient. Ideally, make a note of when particular customers are coming to collect their birds and write down their telephone numbers. Then, if they do not come, they can be given a quick 'phone call as a reminder. A prominent sign outside should be placed in such a way that it can be seen clearly from the road. It should also be obvious when the site is open or closed. It is irritating to drive in only to discover that it is closed.

A car park with adequate turning space will be necessary, with a sign showing where the customers should go to collect their turkeys. It could be that there is a small farm shop on-site, where items such as cranberries, eggs, bunches of sage, milk and cream are also available for those about to embark on cooking the Christmas dinner. Make sure that each customer has your card for future reference. Some producers have also found that providing a recipe leaflet on the best way to cook a turkey is popular.

Finally, it is important to have insurance cover in any enterprise where you are dealing with the public. Again, there are specialist insurance brokers who provide cover for this type of enterprise.

Organic Turkeys

*My brother's turkeys avail themselves much of
the beechmast which they find in his grove.*
(Gilbert White's Journals. 18th Century)

Rearing organic turkeys may be a good option for they attract a premium price and there is a satisfaction in adhering to wholesome traditional standards that are far removed from the mass factory farming undertaken by many big turkey meat producers.

The word *Organic* is a legally defined term so it will be necessary to be registered as an organic producer and to adhere to the required standards. The site will also be subject to inspection by the registration body.

Registration

The European Union has a legal definition of organic that applies to all member countries. It sets minimum standards for organic production and every country within the EU has its own organisation that interprets this law. In the United Kingdom this organisation is *ACOS (Advisory Committee on Organic Standards)*, and is part of *DEFRA*.

ACOS interprets the European Union legislation for organic producers in the UK, but it puts out the job of certification and inspection to certification bodies that are registered with it. Each of these bodies sets its own standards that must not fall below the official requirements but may in some respects exceed them. There is an identifying code for each certification organisation that must be shown on any packaging of their member's produce. They also each have a logo that members can use.

Certification bodies

The best known certifying body is the *Soil Association*, (Code: UK5), with standards that are higher than those specified by *ACOS*. In addition there are seven others that adhere pretty closely to the *UK Organic Standards*. They are:

Organic Farmers and Growers Ltd. (UK2)
Organic Food Federation (UK4)
Organic Trust Ltd. (UK9)
Ascisco Ltd. (UK15)
Scottish Organic Producers' Association (UK3)
Quality Welsh Food Certification Ltd. (UK13)
Irish Organic Farmer's and Growers' Association (UK7)

There is also the *Biodynamic Agricultural Association/Demeter (UK6)* that conforms to minimum UK standards, but with added requirements based on Rudolf Steiner's biodynamic principles. Finally, *CMi Certification (UK10)* provides certification for food processors and suppliers of organic produce.

The prospective organic turkey producer must choose which certification body to register with. The *Soil Association* standards are the oldest and most widely recognised and they recommend principles of husbandry that are more in keeping with traditional small-scale methods of farming practice.

Housing requirements

The basic *UK Organic Standards* permit up to 2500 turkeys in a house, while the *Soil Association* standards specify a maximum number of 250 turkeys.

Perches are desirable and can be provided by placing straw bales in the house. *Soil Association* standards specify a minimum of 40cm per bird of perch space and a maximum of two birds per square metre of housing floor space.

Pasture

Organically reared turkeys need constant access to pasture. This should be well drained and fertile without boggy areas that can harbour disease. Traditional permanent pasture that has never been ploughed but has been properly maintained, has a balance of grasses, clovers and herbs. Most pasture is made up of leys which are part of a rotation system and which are replaced after a few years by another crop as part of a rotation system. In these circumstances, short grasses suitable for poultry can be sown.

If land has not previously been used for organic production, a conversion period of two years is required, although under certain conditions this can be reduced to one year. The planned conversion must be agreed with the chosen certification body. Financial aid is available under the *DEFRA's Organic Entry Level Stewardship Scheme (OELS)*.

UK Organic Standards require a maximum of 1000 turkeys per hectare (2.47 acres), while the *Soil Association* standards specify 800 per hectare.

All the standards require the provision of proper protection from predators and shelter for the birds while they are out on range. The turkeys cannot be slaughtered before they are 140 days old. Potential organic producers are advised to read the book *Organic Poultry*. (See *Reference Section*).

Alternatives to Organic Registration

Organic registration adds an extra cost to turkey production and the small producer might not find the expense worthwhile. The *Soil Association* has a scheme where several small producers in the same area can share the cost, but this may not be applicable.

The *Wholesome Food Association* is an organisation that operates for small producers selling their produce locally. Their standards are equivalent to any

Straw Yard System for a Small Group of Growers or a Breeding Group

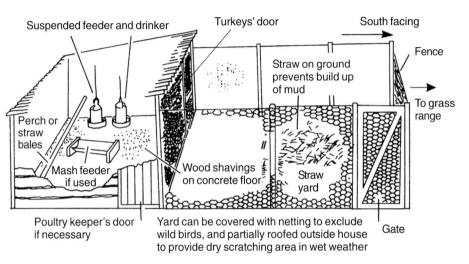

Suspended feeder and drinker — Turkeys' door — South facing — Fence — Straw on ground prevents build up of mud — To grass range — Perch or straw bales — Mash feeder if used — Wood shavings on concrete floor — Straw yard — Poultry keeper's door if necessary — Yard can be covered with netting to exclude wild birds, and partially roofed outside house to provide dry scratching area in wet weather — Gate

official certification body, and often exceed them. There is no system of inspection and it operates on a basis of trust, but as callers can see for themselves under what conditions the turkeys are raised, abusing this trust is unlikely, for any abuse would soon come to light. The *WFA* has branches throughout the UK.

Where small numbers of turkeys are being raised for local customers, they can still be advertised at the farm gate. Although not specifically labelled as organic, which would be a contravention of the regulations, the produce could have a notice stating that the birds are kept humanely, fed on organic feeds and allowed free access to pasture. Customers would soon accept that the birds are organic in everything but name.

There is also the *Freedom Food Association* set up by the *RSPCA* to ensure minimum welfare standards for poultry and livestock. They do not specify either free-range or organic systems as necessities. Registered producers can use the *Freedom Food* logo on their produce packaging.

Free-Range is another term that is defined in law. Birds described as free-range must have continuous access to open air runs and be kept according to the minimum density standards of 1,000 birds per hectare.

Summary of Organic Requirements

Maximum per house: 250	Minimum space in house: 2 birds/sq.m
Maximum per hectare: 800	Minimum perch space: 40cm per bird
Minimum outside: Two thirds of life	Killed: Not before 140 days
Conversion of site: 1-2 years	Outside shelter: Required
Organic feed: Required	Predator protection: Required

(Based on *Soil Association* standards. Basic *UK Standards* may differ)

Janice Houghton-Wallace of *Turkey Club UK* with one of her exhibits at the *Poultry Club of Great Britain's* National Championship Show. *(Katie Thear)*

Floor pens for turkeys are provided at shows. *(Katie Thear)*

Showing Turkeys

The Norfolk Black is a favourite.
(Good Poultry Keeping. C. E. Fermor. 1947)

Turkey breeders who are interested in breeding some of the traditional coloured breeds may wish to exhibit them at poultry shows. Taking part in a show enables entrants to meet other breeders, perhaps to pick up some useful tips, look at their birds and understand more about what factors make up a successful show bird. It is also a good social occasion.

Types of show

There are a great many shows that include poultry. The big ones are the *National Championship Show* and the *Poultry Clubs' Federation Show*. These are held in the winter and as they normally have the top birds on show, are not really for the beginner.

At the next level are the summer *Agricultural Shows* that will normally have a poultry section. The *Championship Shows* are the main regional poultry shows, and below those are the other *Regional Shows* and the small *Voucher Shows* organised by local breed clubs.

At the present time, most of these shows have few if any turkey entries, so check with your local shows to see whether there are any appropriate classes. The *Turkey Club UK* will also be able to advise on this.

Agricultural Shows are usually held over the period of May to September, and Poultry Shows from October to April, so there are always competitions to visit.

Before taking part in a show, it is a good idea to visit one or two in order to see how they work, and to speak with other visitors and participants. It is also an opportunity to appraise the standard of birds being shown.

Turkeys moult during the summer period so this is not a good time for showing. The autumn and winter shows are the ones to go for.

Preparations

Choice of birds

Birds that do well at shows are those that are good examples of their breed, are well grown, healthy and well presented. Therefore, success begins with good husbandry, feeding turkeys correctly, keeping them in the right conditions and ensuring that they have no health problems.

Breeding pens should be of smooth wood surfaces not wire, as tail feathers can be damaged by rubbing against it. From this starting point, the birds

Poultry Shows

National Shows	National Championship Show	Poultry Clubs' Federation Show
Large Regional	Championship Shows	Large Agricultural Shows
Small Regional	Small Agricultural Shows	Breed Club Voucher Shows

The beginner is recommended to start with a small local show before exhibiting at any of the larger national shows

for showing can be selected. They should be fully grown as size and conformation are key points and there should be no deformation of the body, legs or feet. Feather colouring and markings should be correct for the particular breed. The breed standard should be consulted so that a comparison can be drawn between the ideal and the actual. The scale of points against which exhibited birds are marked by the judges is as follows:

Scale of Points for All Breeds

Type, carriage and size	40	
Head	20	
Legs and feet	10	*British Poultry Standards.*
Colour	20	Poultry Club of Great Britain
Condition	10	
	100	

Application

The next step is to send for an application form and return it promptly to the Show Secretary, along with the appropriate fee. This will vary depending on the size and prestige of the show. Application forms are normally required about six weeks before the show date. Take care when filling in the form to ensure that your bird has been entered in the correct category for its type.

Preparing the birds

If your turkeys have been handled and talked to from the outset they are more likely to be tame and settled in show conditions. They can be put into a pen at home well before going to the show so that they are used to being confined. It is easy to make up a pen of timber and hurdles. It needs to be about 120cm square (1.4 sq.m) and have a roof. The front of the pen should be open so that the bird is used to being confined as well as to the noises and bustle of people passing.

Check carefully to make sure that no external parasites have been picked up. This can happen to even the most cared for bird. Washing coloured turkeys is not usually necessary, but if a bird does need a wash, do it at least a week before showing. This gives time for the feathers to regain their natural sheen. Use warm water and soap flakes or baby shampoo, rinse well and dry with a hairdryer on a cool setting. Make sure that you dry with the lie of the feathers, not against otherwise it really will be a 'bad hair day'. Ensure that the birds are returned to a draught-free environment afterwards. It goes without saying that during washing, the wings should be kept confined and it is easier for two people than for one.

Just before the show, give the head, legs and feet a gentle clean with an old toothbrush, and finally rub the legs and the beak with something like *Vaseline* to give them a good finish.

Travelling to the show

Turkeys are large birds and will need a travelling box of an appropriate size. A strong cardboard box with air holes may suffice providing that it is reinforced with something like duck tape. A home-made crate or box is ideal and will last well but it will be heavier. It should be large enough not to constrict the feathers and snug enough so that the bird is not thrown about by the motion of the vehicle.

A travelling box should be about 250cm high so there is sufficient air space. It is sensible to prepare the box first and place it in the back of the vehicle or trailer, then carry the turkey out and place it into the box, talking quietly to it, to minimise any stress.

On arrival at the show, collect the pen numbers from the Secretary and locate your pens, checking that they have already been provided with litter on the floor. Most shows will provide exhibition cages.

A fully-grown turkey, particularly a stag, can be heavy, so it is easier to carry it to the pen by itself, rather than trying to struggle with the box as well. An alternative is to use is a light folding flat trolley. The box can be lifted onto it and wheeled to the pen. This is a good idea if the journey from the car to the pen is a long one, which can happen if other exhibitors' vehicles are blocking the entrance.

Once the bird is in the pen, brush its feathers with a smooth cloth and provide some favourite titbits to help it settle down. Some shows provide water containers but you cannot count on it so take your own, together with a small jug. Again, some shows provide food but it is advisable to take your own so that the birds are eating rations that they are used to.

Take the birds straight home after the show and as soon as possible let them stretch and run about. It is worth delousing them again straightaway in case anything has been picked up. If you should be fortunate to win prize cards or rosettes, display them prominently so that potential buyers of your birds cannot miss them. They will be impressed that you breed turkeys to a good standard, and this will assist you in obtaining the best prices.

Health

Turkeys do not appreciate stuffy, cramped quarters.
(Herbert Howes. 1939)

Maintaining the health of the turkey flock stems from good hygiene and sound management. Most small-scale turkey owners should experience little trouble provided they follow good husbandry procedures. The main points are as follows:

• Always buy healthy vaccinated stock from a known breeder.
• Quarantine new stock for a couple of weeks after arrival.
• Try to keep different ages and breeds separate.
• Provide clean, dry and well-ventilated housing.
• Maintain clean housing and dry floor litter.
• Provide good quality food such as pellets and grain regularly.
• Ensure there is fresh drinking water and insoluble grit at all times.
• Clean feeders and drinkers regularly.
• Feed turkeys where wild birds cannot gain access.
• Make sure that there are no rats in the vicinity.
• Check houses and birds regularly for the presence of mites and lice.
• Avoid overstocking and ensure that the housing has sufficient perch space and floor area for the number of birds.
• Ensure that any utilised grassland is free of poisonous plants and boggy areas and has not previously been used by other poultry or turkeys.
• Rotate pasture regularly.
• Study your turkeys and look out for any unusual behaviour.

What to look out for

• Eye, nasal or vent discharge.
• Lack of coordination, limping or a hunched stance.
• Lethargy, with long periods of sitting or lying around.
• Lack of, or excessive, appetite or thirst.
• Thinness or general loss of condition.

Despite all precautions, problems can appear, although they are unlikely in a small-scale non-intensive turkey enterprise. If any bird shows unusual symptoms, isolate it from the rest of the flock in a small pen just in case it is infectious. Provide food and water and keep an eye on it. If several birds are affected, call the vet without delay. There are some diseases that are notifiable; the law requires that you seek veterinary help so that they can be reported. Bear in mind that some diseases can also affect humans (zoonoses) so always wash your hands after contact with the birds.

Good ventilation in the house is a key factor in maintaining flock health. *(Katie Thear)*

The annual moult

The annual moult is not a health condition but a normal manifestation where old feathers are dropped, to be replaced by new ones. However, it is a time when extra care is needed at a time when the bird is under stress and its resources are concentrated on growing new feathers. It needs adequate feeding, so ensure that it is getting enough protein, as in a good quality proprietary feed. It is also a time to check that feather-pecking is not taking place, or in case external parasites have become established. The moult should not last more than around three weeks. If it does, there may be a problem with any of the above-mentioned. (See *External Parasites* Page 84).

Worming

Free-ranging birds are susceptible to internal, parasitic worms, although allowing growers to access clean pasture only will help to avoid infestation. (See *Internal Parasites* Page 86).

Breeding stock kept for several years are particularly at risk so need to be wormed at least once in a season. All worms can be treated with *Flubenvet* added to the food or with *Solubenol* added to the water. Follow the manufacturers' instructions and do not allow the birds to go out on range until the treatment has had time to take effect and has come to an end.

Diseases affecting turkeys

The following diseases are the most common ones that can affect turkeys.

Aspergillosis (Fungal pneumonia)

Aspergillosis fumigatus fungus is the cause of this disease. It is found in mouldy litter, hay or feed. When the spores are inhaled the fungus grows in the lungs. Young birds are most at risk. Poor brooder and hatchery conditions can cause it, hence the common name of 'brooder pneumonia'. Humans can also be affected when it is called 'farmer's lung'. Symptoms are gasping and rapid breathing. Anti-fungal treatments are available but they are expensive. The best approach is prevention.

Avian influenza

Commonly known as bird 'flu, this is caused by a virus and is normally carried by airborne particles from the respiratory tract, as well as by bird droppings or people carrying it on their feet or equipment. This is why it is a good idea to have a container with antiseptic liquid and a brush for cleaning boots or equipment before entering the turkeys' area.

There are many different strains, and common symptoms include discharge from the nostrils, or swollen head and neck in more virulent strains. Most birds recover from mild strains, having then developed an immunity. When it is followed by sinusitis, which is caused by a bacterium, an antibiotic from the vet will help to clear it.

Virulent strains such as H5N1 are killers and must be notified to the authorities. If birds start to die, contact the vet immediately. As is the case with all livestock or pets, it is advisable to wash your hands immediately after handling turkeys whether they are healthy or not. Many people wear gloves when handling them because this also protects the hands from the sharp claws. (See page 7).

Where a virulent strain is discovered, the site will be quarantined and the birds slaughtered, with appropriate compensation paid to commercial sites. *DEFRA* will also issue advice that all poultry should be kept under cover until the threat is over. Covering pens with 25mm gauge netting will ensure that wild birds are excluded.

Blackhead (Histomoniasis)

A once common disease in turkeys it is now rare. It is caused by a protozoan parasite in the liver or caeca. It is usually picked up from land that has been previously grazed by chickens. The parasite is in the eggs of the caecum worm passed in the droppings of the chickens. Turkeys that have access to ground previously used by chickens can pick up the parasite even several years after chickens have left the site.

Symptoms include lethargy, drooping stance, lack of appetite and yellow

Rats carry disease as well as contaminating feed. *(Sorex)*

droppings. Prevention is the best policy, keeping turkeys well away from anywhere that has been in contact with chickens. Blackhead is likely to kill young birds very quickly, so act at once if it is suspected. An antibiotic can be added to the water and should solve the problem.

Coccidiosis
This is normally seen in young birds, and results from a protozoan parasite picked up from droppings. Good hygiene is essential in maintaining clean dry litter, as the coccidia oocysts can be brought in on muddy boots. By the same token it is not advisable to run the birds on ground that has been previously stocked by turkeys, or which is particulalrly wet.

Symptoms are loss of appetite, birds looking cold and droopy and with white or bloody droppings. It is most likely to crop up after wet weather if the birds are out on range. This is a fast acting disease that kills, so call the vet immediately. Turkey feeds can include anti–coccidials that can do much to prevent the disease. A recovering flock can be given multivitamins for a week after veterinary treatment to build up their health.

Erysipelas
Unusual in small flocks, this is a disease that is soil-borne and can enter through damaged areas of the skin. It is common in sheep and pigs. Symptoms include listlessness; a swollen head, neck, joints and snood and there can be sudden death. This is a zoonotic disease transferable to humans, and the vet should be notified. Treatment is with antibiotics.

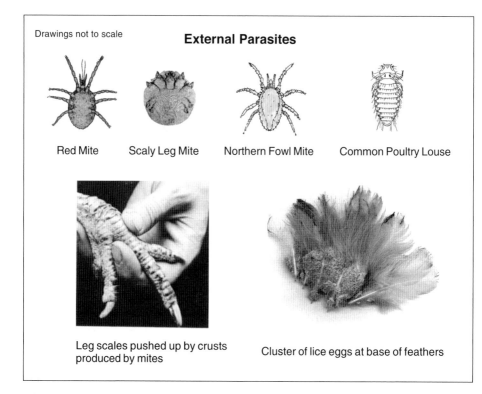

Drawings not to scale

External Parasites

Red Mite   Scaly Leg Mite   Northern Fowl Mite   Common Poultry Louse

Leg scales pushed up by crusts produced by mites

Cluster of lice eggs at base of feathers

External parasites

Lice

Lice can be seen on adult turkeys but are unlikely to be found on growing poults. They are about 2mm long and a yellow/brown colour. Lice are found on the skin particularly around the vent, and they lay eggs that adhere to the skin with a sticky substance around the base of the feathers.

Lice are a constant irritant to the birds and they can become listless and ill-tempered leading to outbreaks of fighting. Deal with the birds individually by removing the egg clusters and disposing of them. Sprinkle louse powder under the tail around the vent area, under the wings between the legs and on the back. Rub it well in and repeat the treatment a week later to kill off any newly hatched lice.

Red Mite *(Dermanyssus gallinae)*

These hide in house crevices during the day and feed on the birds at night. They are about 1mm long and grey in colour, although those that have sucked blood will be red. They are almost certainly introduced by wild birds. Turkeys badly bitten by mites can become anaemic and jaundiced and may begin to lose weight.

Dusting against external parasites. *(Katie Thear)*

If the situation is left untreated, turkeys may begin to die. Treat the house during the daytime. Spray all cracks in the house and the underside of perches with an appropriate treatment and repeat a week later. I have also used a blowlamp when the house is empty. This is effective providing you don't start a fire! If the turkeys are perching on straw bales, spray these too. If the infestation does not clear up quickly, remove the straw bales and replace them with fresh ones.

Northern Mite
These are like lice in that they live entirely on their host. They are about 1mm long and grey in colour. Unlike red mite, they can be seen on the bird during the day. The symptoms are similar to birds infested with red mite. They are difficult to eradicate, so thorough and repeated treatment of each bird will be necessary.

Scaly Leg Mite *(Sarcoptes mutans)*
This is an annoying mite that finds its way between the leg scales. Its activities produce white crusts that push up and distort the scales, making the legs look unsightly. It is extremely infectious and where birds are affected, they need immediate treatment, while litter and any straw bales should be burned and replaced.

It is important not to pull the crusts away other-wise the scales will be torn off as well, leaving an open wound. It is best to soak the legs in warm soapy water first so that the crusts come away without causing damage. After they are dried, the legs can then be treated with a proprietary mite killer. A second application should be ap-plied a week later to deal with any subsequent hatchings. In my experience, painting on Benzyl benzoate is extremely effective in dealing with the mites.

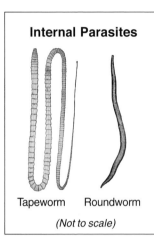

Internal Parasites

Tapeworm   Roundworm
(Not to scale)

Internal Parasites
There are several different types of worms that can affect turkeys. They can be picked up from the ground when the turkeys are out on range. Putting growing poults onto fresh ground helps but the droppings of wild birds can introduce the eggs of these internal parasites onto otherwise clean pasture. (See *Worming* Page 81).

Caecal Worms
Sometimes called hairworms these build up in the blind gut or caecum.

Gapeworms
These attach themselves to the windpipe causing the bird to stretch out its neck to help it to breathe.

Roundworms
Both large and small roundworms infest and lay their eggs in the intestines. The worms absorb nutrients from the food so consequently the turkey can develop a great appetite. If the infestation grows worse the bird will look pale and stop growing.

Tapeworms
Tapeworms attach themselves to the lining of the intestinal tract. As the worm grows sections break off and eggs are passed in the droppings. These eggs are harmless to turkeys but if they are eaten by insects such as beetles, they hatch within their host. If the insect is then eaten by a turkey, the tapeworm infestation will be transmitted.

Newcastle Disease (Fowl Pest)
This disease has been practically eliminated from the UK through a nation-wide vaccination programme. It can occasionally crop up so it is still advis-able to know about it because it is a very serious illness.

The first symptoms are similar to gapeworm, with birds stretching their neck and gasping for breath. The birds begin to die in 24 hours, and in in-creasing numbers. Contact the vet at once for it is a notifiable disease.

Even the best turkey can look scruffy when it is in moult. *(Katie Thear)*

Pasteurella (Fowl Cholera)

This is a dangerous and highly infectious disease that is rare these days and very unlikely to occur in a small-scale enterprise with a good hygiene regime. Symptoms include listlessness, loss of appetite, discharge from the nostrils and diarrhoea, quickly followed by dead birds.

It can be contracted through the drinking water so it is important not only that the turkeys always have fresh water, but that the water containers are always kept clean.

A major breakout of this disease may require the whole flock to be culled. Once this is done the house and ground used by the flock must be thoroughly cleaned and disinfected and kept free of turkeys for a year or two.

Salmonella

There are many strains of salmonella in poultry, several of which can infect turkeys. Young poults are particularly vulnerable. They become listless and have no appetite for food. Prevention is the best option; buy poults from a reliable source and practise strict hygiene.

With a good hygiene regime there is little likelihood of a salmonella infection arising. They are bacterial infections and where they do appear, can be treated with antibiotics added to the drinking water. Contact the vet if this disease is suspected so that the most suitable treatment can be administered.

Sinusitis (Mycoplasma gallisepticum)

This is a respiratory bacterial infection (Mg), that is highly infectious but rarely fatal. Symptoms are a discharge from the nostrils and eyes, and coughs and sneezes. Mucus can sometimes be observed on a wing where the bird has wiped its eye. Poor ventilation in the turkey house provides suitable conditions for an outbreak. The vet will advise on the best treatment.

Mycoplasma synoviae (Ms), is similar but also includes swelling in the joints, lameness, breast blisters, and loss of weight. This condition can be largely prevented by buying stock from a reliable source. Treatment is similar to *Mycoplasma gallisepticum*. There are other Mycoplasma strains but they are unlikely to be seen in small and well managed flocks. Bear in mind, however, that any respiratory infection should be notified to the vet.

Other Problems

Crop binding (Pendulous crop)

A bird can become crop-bound where food stays and builds up in the crop causing it to swell up. This can result from a feeding problem such as eating dry grass or excessive drinking in very hot weather, but it is more likely to be caused by a fungal infection that starts to block the pathway from the crop to the stomach. It is important to deal with it early on before it becomes too acute as the crop can become diseased.

To clear the crop, up-end the turkey then stroke the crop to expel the liquid gently through the beak. Isolate the bird onto a clean area, with just water, medicated to clear the infection. After a couple of days feed a little grain, then normal feeding can be gradually reintroduced and the bird returned to the flock. This condition is most likely to occur in grown birds rather than poults. It is also more common in hot weather and occurs more in stags than hens. It can also be an inherited condition, where a recessive gene produces a distended crop in which liquid tends to accumulate. (See page 19). It would be inadvisable to breed from any bird with this condition.

Foot problems

Mud can dry and adhere to the foot, building up to a hard lump on the underside. Of course, turkeys should not be allowed to walk about in muddy conditions, but if this problem does arise the foot will need cleaning. The mud is likely to be very hard so do not try to pull or pick it off which could damage the underside of the foot. Place the foot in warm water and soften the mud ball until it all comes away. It can take quite a time to remove it all.

The foot can also be penetrated by something sharp and become infected causing lameness. Clean the affected area with warm water and gently squeeze out any pus. The wound can then be dried and sprayed with antiseptic. Place the bird on clean bedding for a couple of days for the condition to clear up. If the foot is still swollen and feels hot then it is infected and will need antibiotics to clear it up. Such infections can also arise from the bird being kept in unhygenic conditions underfoot. Redness on the footpads is usually the result of ammonia burns from old and damp litter. Change it frequently and keep it well raked.

Leg and wing problems

Poults with straddled legs can have the condition for a number of reasons. Ensure that they are on a surface where their feet can grip and not slide out from under them when they are first put into a brooder. This condition, as well as that of crooked toes, can also be the result of a deficiency disease inherited from the breeding stock. This is why it is important to give breeding birds a purpose-produced breeder ration.

Lameness in adult birds can result from a vitamin deficiency or lack of phosphorus in the diet. A deficiency of manganese in the diet can also result in a form of lameness known as *Perosis* or slipped tendon. If these conditions are spotted early, the diet can be amended to solve the problem. However if this type of lameness is not cured, the bird should be culled. If the dietary management is sound, none of the deficiency conditions are likely to occur.

Turkeys can also contract scaly leg mite. This is dealt with earlier under *External Parasites*.

Turkeys can panic fairly easily, even when they are well grown, and may be knocked down and injured. If an adult bird breaks a leg and it is a clean break, a lightweight splint may solve the problem. This can be removed when the leg has healed. If a wing breaks, there is little that can be done apart from taping it to the side of the bird. Remove and replace the tape regularly until the wing repairs. This may not work but it is worth a go if the turkey is a good breeder. A vet will obviously advise as to the best course of action.

Poisoning

This is an unlikely occurrence but birds can be poisoned by plants or seeds while on range. There are many poisonous plants but the most common are as follows: Corncockle, Foxglove, Laburnum, Laurel, Milkweed, Deadly Nightshade, Thornapple, Yew.

It is always a good idea to have a good book on the subject of poisonous plants so that identification is simplified.

Wounds

The most common wounds arise from tearing of the hen's skin from the stag's claws. Breeding females can be fitted with a 'saddle' which protects them from being injured by mounting stags. The stags should also have their claws clipped and the spurs kept filed down. Another source of wounds comes from feather pecking, where birds are too confined, bored or their diet is inadequate. Whatever the cause, injured birds must be separated from the flock, the wounds cleaned and antiseptic spray applied.

The Turkey Year

Spring - March, April and May

Breeding Flock

Eggs Collect often, keep records and put the best eggs into store for later incubation. Check that the incubator is clean and running normally. Incubate batches of eggs as they become available. Candle all eggs after 7 days and reject the infertile ones. After hatching, clean and sterilise the incubator before starting the next batch.

Poults Prepare the brood area for the newly hatched poults. After hatching, transfer them to the brooder, putting them under a heat lamp. Provide chick crumbs and water and protect them from draughts and vermin. At six weeks old transfer them to a rearing area for growing on and gradually change over to grower's pellets. Take orders for selling surplus poults.

Breeding pens Ensure that there is always clean litter, and that all pens have breeder's pellets, water and grit, together with nest boxes and low perches. Change stags regularly, and remove hens with unwanted broodiness to a cool isolation coop until they are ready to rejoin the flock.

Outside Both growers and breeding birds can go out into the fresh air as soon as the weather is suitable. For a straw yard, check fencing and lay down fresh clean straw beforehand. On range, check that the ground is dry and free of poisonous plants. Check the protective fencing and make sure that there are adequate windbreaks and sheltered areas. Move the outside feeders and drinkers regularly, worm the turkeys as necessary and if they are particularly flighty, wing clip them, although tall fences are preferable.

Christmas Turkeys

Order six week-old poults for delivery in July. For delivery of day old chicks in May, prepare brooder conditions beforehand and rear as described above.

Summer - June, July and August

Breeding Flock

Eggs Continue to collect eggs, record them, and set the best for incubation. Run succeeding batches through the incubator and rear the new chicks under heat for six weeks. Do not forget to candle newly introduced eggs after seven days and remove those that are not fertile.

Poults Do not mix batches of different ages. Sell any surplus poults outside your immediate area. Maintain a high level of hygiene, rearing poults on clean and disinfected areas protected from vermin. Scrub out feeders and drinkers regularly and maintain fresh litter in inside areas.

Outside Move outside birds onto fresh ground as necessary. Check birds for worms, mites and lice and treat them promptly if needed. Provide plenty of fresh water in hot weather when consumption goes up. Select future breeding stock and identify them with tags or leg rings. Keep up feed protein levels during the moulting period and keep an extra watch for feather pecking at this time.

Christmas Turkeys

Continue to hatch fertile eggs and raise new chicks. Move six week-old poults off heat to a rearing area and change over to a grower's ration. Alternatively, take delivery of six week-old poults and put them into a prepared rearing pen. Do not mix different batches of birds. Begin promotion for Christmas turkey sales.

Autumn - September, October and November

Breeding Flock

Make final selection of future breeding stock. If showing birds, send in first show entries in September and October. Prepare the show birds with some pen training. Continue to let birds out during fine weather. Ensure that fences and houses are secure as the weather grows colder. Take action against rats. Worm breeding stock.

Christmas Turkeys

Continue to take orders for oven-ready birds from farm gate customers and 'long-legged' ones from local burchers. Switch feed to a finisher ration for the final weeks if required. Increase rations to the growing birds, continue to raise the height of the feeders and drinkers and introduce extra ones if necessary. Keep clean litter on the ground. Continue to check for mites and lice, and let the birds out into the fresh air during suitable conditions. Make all preparations for slaughter in December. Remove and slaughter those birds that finish in November. Store these in the freezer after plucking, eviscerating and dressing.

Winter - December, January and February

Breeding Flock

Maintain vigilant action against both vermin and predators during the cold months. Make sure that all birds have sufficient food during the cold weather. Clean and check the incubator. From February, move birds into breeding pens, start providing artificial light and switch feed to a breeder's ration.

Christmas Turkeys

Guard against two legged poachers. Slaughter, pluck, hang and dress birds during December. Sell the finished turkeys to customers. Afterwards, clean and disinfect everything and everywhere where the birds have been. Relax and enjoy Christmas! There's time for a winter holiday after that, too.

Reference Section

Books

Codes of Recommendation for the Welfare of Livestock: Turkeys. MAFF. 1987.
Turkeys. Bulletin 67. MAFF. 1959
Profit from Turkeys. Katie Thear. Broad Leys Publishing. 1981.
Turkeys and Geese. Herbert Howes. Macmillan. 1949.
Raising Turkeys. Morley Jull. McGraw-Hill. 1947.
Raising Your Own Turkeys. Leonard Mercia. Storey Publishing. 1981
Turkeys: A Gude to Management. David Bland. Crowood Press. 2000.
Turkeys at Home. Michael Roberts. Domestic Fowl Trust. 1989.
Organic Poultry. Katie Thear. Broad Leys Publishing. 2005
Incubation. Katie Thear. Broad Leys Publishing. 2003
British Poultry Standards. Victoria Roberts. Poultry Club of Great Britain. 1997

Organisations

ACOS (Advisory Committee on Organic Standards).
Email:organic.standards@defra.gsi.gov.uk
Anglian Turkey Association. Tel: 01621 815740.
DEFRA. Helpline: 08459 335577. Publications: 08459 556000.
Farmfresh Turkey Association. www.golden-promise.co.uk
FAWC (Farm Animal Welfare Council). Tel: 020 7904 6531.
Freedom Food Ltd. Tel: 08707 540014. www.rspca.org.uk
Humane Slaughter Association. Tel: 01582 831919. www.hsa.org.uk
National Association of Farmers' Markets. Tel: 08454 588420. www.farmersmarkets.net
Organic Farmers and Growers Ltd. Tel: 01743 440512. www.organicfarmers.uk.com
Poultry Club of Great Britain. Tel: 01476 550067. www.poultryclub.org
Rare Breeds Survival Trust. Tel: 02476 696551. www.rare-breeds.com
The Soil Association. Tel: 0117 914 2406. www.soilassociation.org
The Wholesome Food Association. Tel: 01237 441118. www.wholesome-food.org.uk
Turkey Club UK. Tel: 01988 600763. www.turkeyclub.org.uk

Suppliers

Stock

Atwells. Tel: 01527 66191.
Baron Turkeys. Tel: 01928 716416.
British United Turkeys. Tel: 01244 661111. www.but.co.uk
CEF Chicks (UK). Tel: 01704 840980.
Copas Traditional Turkeys. Tel: 01628 474678. www.copasturkeys.co.uk
Cottage Farm Turkeys. Tel: 01959 532506.
Cuddy Farms. Tel: 01560 482404. www.cuddyfarms.com
Cyril Bason (Stokesay) Ltd. Tel: 01588 673204. www.cyril-bason.co.uk
Friars Close Farm Turkeys. Tel: 01832 273357.
Highline Turkeys. Tel: 01584 861401.
Holly Berry Hatcheries. Tel: 01522 754388.
Kelly Turkey Farms. Tel: 01245 223581. www.kellyturkeys.com
Leicestershire Farm Fresh Turkeys. Tel: 01162 595285.
Lloyd Pennine Poultry. Tel: 01522 778722. www.lloydpoultry.com
Payne's Turkeys. Tel: 01430 872455. www.paynesturkeys.co.uk
Peele's Norfolk Black Turkeys. Tel: 01362 850237.

Ponderosa. Tel: 01425 672194.
SCF (Turkeys). Tel: 0151 339 2543.

Housing
APS Mobile Poultry Units. Tel: 01822 860471.
ARM Buildings Ltd. Tel: 01889 650274. www.armbuildings.co.uk
Cosikennels Ltd. Tel: 01953 718294. www.cosiarks.com
McGregor Poultry Housing. Tel: 01962 772368. www.mcgregorpolytunnels.co.uk
NFP Ledbury. Tel: 01531 631020. www.freerange.org
Smiths Sectional Buildings. Tel: 01630 673747. www.smithssectionalbuildings.co.uk

Equipment
Ascott Smallholding Supplies Ltd. Tel: 0845 130 6285. www.ascott.biz
Danro Ltd. (Labels). Tel: 01455 847061/2. www.danroltd.co.uk
Domestic Fowl Trust. Tel: 01386 833083 www.domesticfowltrust.co.uk
Hengrave Feeders Ltd. Tel: 01284 704803.
Parkland Products Ltd. (Outside feeders). Tel: 01797 270399. www.parklandproducts.co.uk
Rooster Booster. (12volt lighting system). Tel: 01963 345279. www.roosterbooster.co.uk
Solway Feeders Ltd. (Slaughtering and plucking equipment). Tel: 01557 500253.
www.solwayfeeders.com

Incubators
Aliwal Incubators. Tel: 01508 481729.
Ascott Smallholding Supplies Ltd. Tel: 0845 130 6285. www.ascott.biz
Brinsea Products Ltd. Tel: 0845 226 0120. www.brinsea.co.uk
Hatch-it Incubators. Tel: 01635 230238. www.hatchitincubators.com
Interhatch. Tel: 01246 264646.
MS Incubators. Tel: 0116 247 8335.
S & T Poultry. Tel: 01945 585618.
Solway Feeders Ltd. Tel: 01557 500253. www.solwayfeeders.com

Free-Range and Organic Feeds
BOCM Pauls Ltd. Tel: 01757 244000. www.bocmpauls.co.uk
Hi-Peak Feeds. Tel: 01142 480608. www.hipeak.co.uk
SmallHolder Feeds. Tel: 01362 822900. www.smallholderfeed.co.uk
W.H. Marriage & Sons Ltd. Tel: 01245 612000. www.marriagefeeds.co.uk

Electric Fencing
Electric Fencing Direct Ltd. Tel: 0870 609 2076. www.electricfencing.co.uk
G. A. & M. Strange. Tel: 01225 891236.
Kiwi Fencing. Tel: 01728 688005. www.kiwifencing.co.uk
Rappa Electric Fencing. Tel: 01624 810665. www.rappa.co.uk

Vermin Control
DuPont Animal Health Solutions. Tel: 0800 316 8060. www.ahs.dupont.com
Ilex Organics Ltd. Tel: 01673 885175. www.ilexorganics.com
Pelgar International Ltd. Tel: 01420 80744. www.getthatrat.com
Sorex Ltd. Tel: 0151 420 7151. www.sorex.com

Insurance
Cliverton Insurance. Tel: 0845 075 2011. www.cliverton.co.uk
Greenlands Smallholder's Insurance. Tel: 01970 702010. www.greenlands.co.uk
Ottery Insurance Services. Tel: 0800 018 3495. www.ottery.co.uk
Stuart Benger & Co. Tel: 01743 462277. www.stuartbenger.co.uk

Glossary of Turkey Terms

Ash: The mineral component of feed.

As hatched (AH): Where no attempt has been made to sex poults.

Barring: Stripes of alternate light and dark colours across feathers.

Beard (or Tassel): Tuft of coarse, dark, hairlike feathers projecting from breast.

Breeder: Male or female kept for breeding purposes.

Breeding saddle: A cover to protect the hen's sides from the stag's claws at mating.

Brooder: Protected area with artificial heat for raising poults.

Broody: A hen showing signs of wanting to sit on and incubate a clutch of eggs.

Candler: Source of bright light to examine internal egg contents.

Cape: Feathers at back of neck and between shoulders.

Carriage: Body shape and stance, important in show requirements and selection of breeders.

Caruncles: Fleshy growths on head and wattles.

Coverts: Covering feathers on wings and tail.

Crop: Area of lower gullet where food is temporarily stored before passing to gizzard.

Dimple breast: Cleft between two sides of breast, usually indicating a good meat bird.

Display: Male courtship ritual with raised tail feathers and strutting walk.

Dressing: Presenting the eviscerated bird to its best advantage as oven-ready.

Drumming: Characteristic two-note sound produced by male as part of courtship display.

Drumstick: Tibia or lower thigh, as referred to in a meat bird.

Dustbath: Area of fine earth where birds 'bathe', allowing earth to sift between feathers.

Egg sanitant: Antiseptic solution for ensuring that hatching eggs are free of pathogens.

Evisceration: Removing guts and other offal from slaughtered birds.

Feed Conversion Ratio (FCR): Ratio of food eaten in relation to liveweight of bird.

Genotype: The genetic makeup of a bird. (See also Phenotype).

Gizzard: Area of digestive system where grains are ground down with the help of grit..

Gobble: Sound made by male turkey.

Gobbler: Alternative name for male turkey (USA).

Hen: Adult female.

Hock: Joint between lower thigh and shank.

Jake: Immature male (USA).

Keel: Breastbone or sternum.

Litter: Floor covering such as wood shavings.

Liveweight: Weight of live bird, as distinct from weight of oven-ready bird.

Long-legged: Slaughtered and plucked but uneviscerated birds that also retain head and feet.

Moult: Seasonal loss of old feathers to be replaced by new ones.

Notifiable disease: One whose existence must be reported to the authorities.

Phenotype: The physical type as seen outwardly. (See also Genotype).

Poult: Chick or young bird.

Preening: Grooming the feathers to keep them in good condition.

Primaries: Main flight or quill feathers at wing tips.

Secondaries: Secondary flight feathers of wings.

Shank: Area of leg between foot and hock joint.

Skirt: Feathers hanging down on either side of tail.

Snood: Fleshy appendage growing from forehead and hanging over the beak.

Stag: Adult male

Standard: Template of ideal external features for a particular breed.

Strain: Number of birds from same family group, developed for a particular characteristic.

Stubs: Stubs of feathers left after plucking. Their removal is referred to as 'stubbing'.

Trap Nest: Nest allows hen to go in but not out until released, so that egg details can be recorded.

Tom: American term for an adult male.

Uropygium: 'Parson's nose', the protuberance from which tail feathers grow.

Wattles: Fleshy appendages growing from the throat.

Wing clipping: Clipping of primary feathers on one wing of flighty birds.

Withdrawal period: Time required to elapse after medication of bird before meat can be sold.

Wry tail: Tail that is crooked to the right or left.

Zoonoses: Ailments that can also affect humans.

Index